Book & CD for B♭, E♭, Bass Clef and C instruments

PLAY 8 SONGS WITH A PROFESSIONAL BAND

## HOW TO USE THE CD:

Each song has two tracks:

**1) Full Stereo Mix**

**All recorded instruments** are present on this track.

**2) Split Track**

**Bass** parts can be removed
by turning down the volume on the LEFT channel.

**Guitar** parts can be removed
by turning down the volume on the RIGHT channel.

Cover photo: Torben Dragsby / © Authentic Hendrix, LLC

ISBN 978-1-4584-0269-1

Exclusively Distributed By

7777 W. Bluemound Rd. P.O. Box 13819 Milwaukee, WI 53213

For all works contained herein:
Unauthorized copying, arranging, adapting, recording, Internet posting, public performance,
or other distribution of the printed or recorded music in this publication is an infringement of copyright.
Infringers are liable under the law.

Visit Hal Leonard Online at
**www.halleonard.com**

# Jimi Hendrix®

BOOK



CD

**CD TRACK**

1 Full Stereo Mix

9 Split Mix

C Version

# Fire

Words and Music by
Jimi Hendrix

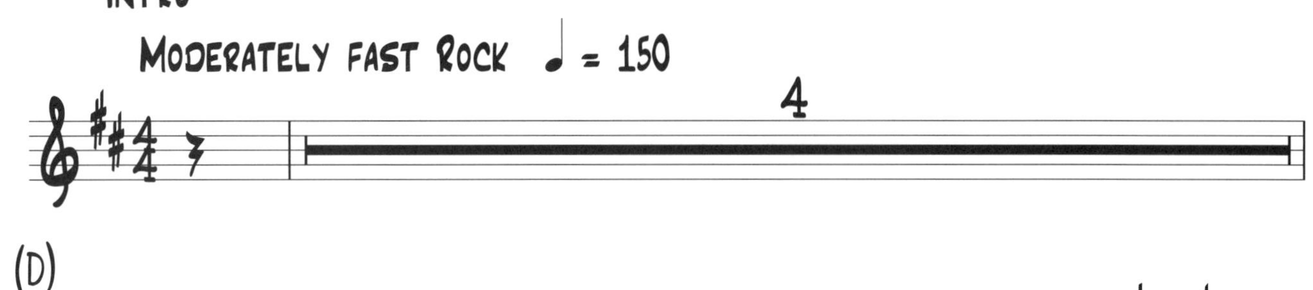

Copyright © 1967, 1968, 1980 by EXPERIENCE HENDRIX, L.L.C.
Copyright Renewed 1995, 1996
All Rights Controlled and Administered by EXPERIENCE HENDRIX, L.L.C.
All Rights Reserved

To Coda
Dadd 9
Cadd 9
Dadd 9
Cadd 9
BA - BY!
LET ME STAND.
LET ME STAND _ NEXT TO YOUR FIRE! _
LET ME STAND _ NEXT TO YOUR
1.
N.C. (D)
YEAH, _ BA - BY!
LIS-TEN HERE, BA - BY,
FIRE!) _
AND STOP ACT-ING SO CRA-ZY.
2. YOU SAY YOUR
2.
BRIDGE
D
OH! _ MOVE O - VER, _
Cadd 9
ROV - ER, _
AND LET JIM - I TAKE O - VER!
A
C
8VA
YEAH, YOU KNOW WHAT I'M TALK-ING _ 'BOUT!
YEAH! _
LOCO
GUITAR SOLO
N.C. (E)
8
INTERLUDE
N.C.
GET ON WITH IT, BA - BY!
THAT'S WHAT I'M TALK-ING 'BOUT. _
NOW, DIG THIS!
(D)
D.S. AL CODA
HA!
NOW LIS-TEN, BA-BY!
3. YOU TRY TO

Additional Lyrics

2. You say your mum ain't home, it ain't my concern.
Just a play with me, and you won't get burned.
I have only one a itching desire,
Let me stand next to your fire!

3. You try to gimme your money, you better save it babe,
Save it for your rainy day.
I have only one a burning desire,
Let me stand next to your fire!

CD TRACK

2 Full Stereo Mix

10 Split Mix

C Version

# Foxey Lady

Words and Music by
Jimi Hendrix

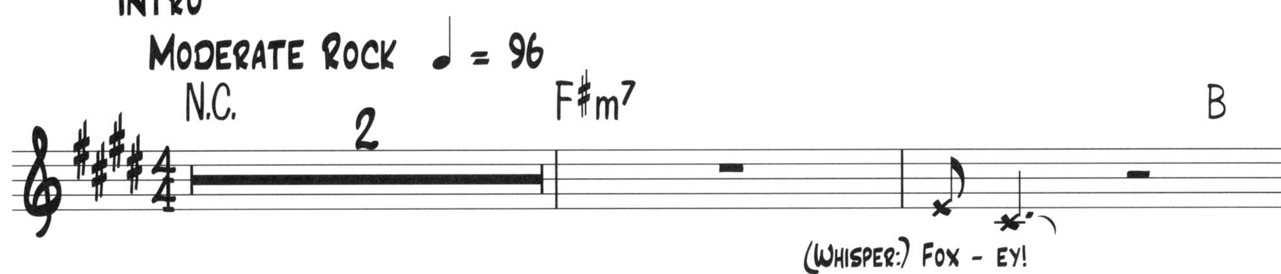


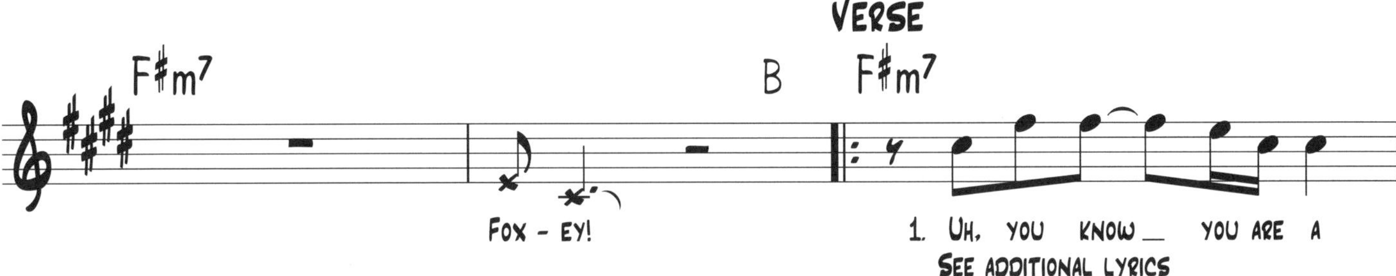

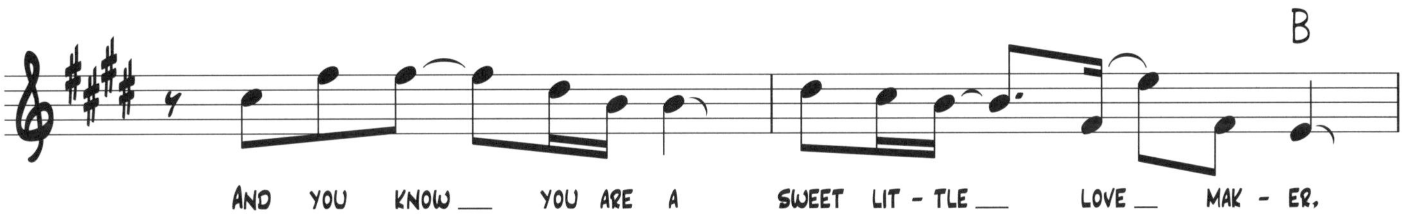


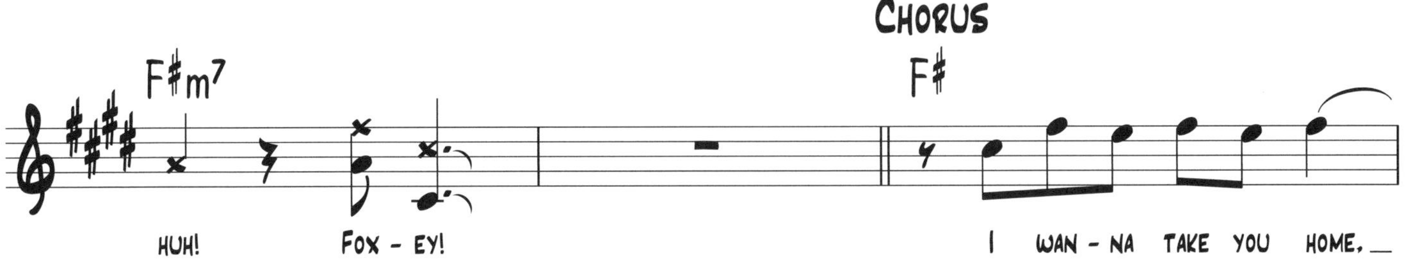

Copyright © 1967, 1968, 1980 by EXPERIENCE HENDRIX, L.L.C.
Copyright Renewed 1995, 1996
All Rights Controlled and Administered by EXPERIENCE HENDRIX, L.L.C.
All Rights Reserved

F#m7 E N.C.(B) F# N.C.
YOU'VE GOT TO BE ALL MINE, ALL MINE. OOH! FOX-EY LA-DY!
1.
F#m7 F#7#9 N.C. F#m7
YEAH! (WHISPER:) FOX-EY!
B
FOX-EY! 2. NOW A
2.
HERE I COME!
GUITAR SOLO
F#m7
FOX-EY LA-DY! FOX-EY LA-DY!
FOX-EY! FOX-EY! FOX-EY! YEAH!
CHORUS
F# E N.C.(B) F#
I'M GON-NA TAKE YOU HOME. UH, HUH! I WON'T DO YOU NO HARM,
E N.C.(B) F# E N.C.(B)
NO. YOU'VE GOT TO BE ALL MINE, ALL MINE.
FREE TIME
F# N.C.
FOX-EY LA-DY! HERE I COME, BA-BY. I'M COM-IN' TO GET YA!

Additional Lyrics

2. Now I see you, come on down on the scene. Oh foxey.
You make me wanna get up and scream! Foxey!
Oh, baby, listen now.

Chorus I've made up my mind.
I'm tired of wasting all my precious time.
You've got to be all mine, all mine.
Foxey lady!
Here I come!

CD TRACK

3 Full Stereo Mix

11 Split Mix

C Version

# Jam 292

Words and Music by
Jimi Hendrix

Intro
Moderate Shuffle ♩. = 106

Riff 1/Guitar Solo (2nd/3rd times)

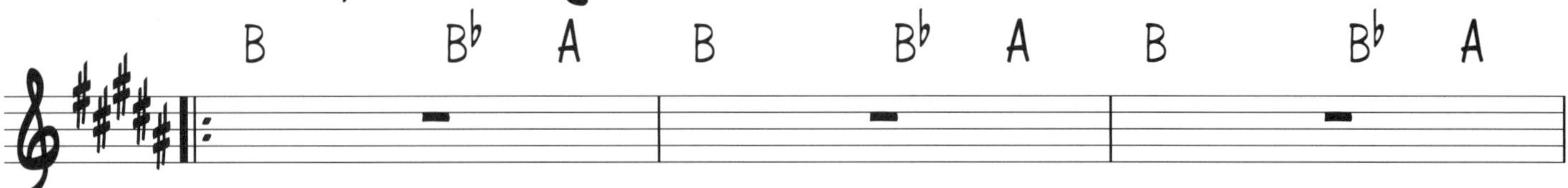


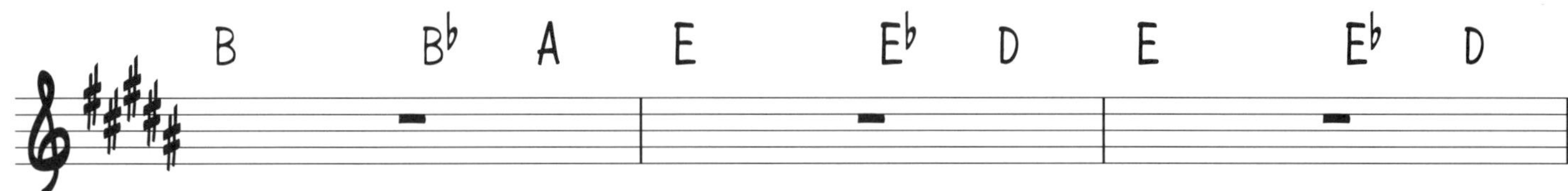

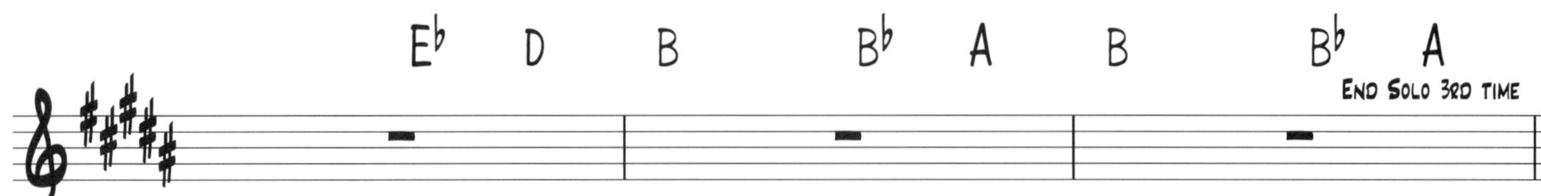


Riff 2

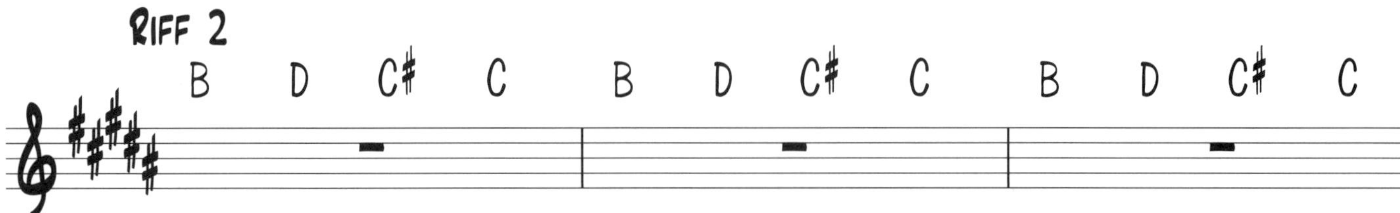



Copyright © 1973 by EXPERIENCE HENDRIX, L.L.C.
Copyright Renewed 2001
All Rights Controlled and Administered by EXPERIENCE HENDRIX, L.L.C.
All Rights Reserved

B D C♯ C E G F♯ F E G F♯ F
B D C♯ C B D C♯ C F♯ A G♯ G
E G F♯ F B D C♯ C B D C♯ C
Riff 3
B7 3 E7 B7
F♯7 E7 B7
Riff 4
B7 3 E7 B7
F♯7 E7 B7
Play 3 times
Guitar Solo 2/Riff 4
B7 3 E7 B7
F♯7 E7 B7
Outro
B7 2
Play 3 times

CD TRACK

4 Full Stereo Mix

12 Split Mix

C Version

# Little Wing

Words and Music by
Jimi Hendrix

Copyright © 1968 by EXPERIENCE HENDRIX, L.L.C.
Copyright Renewed 1996
All Rights Controlled and Administered by EXPERIENCE HENDRIX, L.L.C.
All Rights Reserved

G
Am
Em
WITH A THOU - SAND SMILES
SHE GIVES TO ME FREE.
Bm
B♭
Am
C
IT'S AL - RIGHT, SHE SAID, IT'S AL-RIGHT,
TAKE AN - Y - THING YOU WANT
G
Fadd9
C
FROM ME,
AN - Y - THING,
D
GUITAR SOLO
Em
AN - Y - THING.
G
Am
Em
FLY ON, LIT-TLE WING.
Bm
B♭
Am
C
G
Fadd9
C
D
OUTRO
Em
G
Am
Em
YEAH, YEAH, YEAH, LIT-TLE WING.
Bm
B♭
Am
C
G
Fadd9
C
D

CD TRACK
5 Full Stereo Mix
13 Split Mix
C Version

# Red House

Words and Music by
Jimi Hendrix

Copyright © 1967, 1968, 1980 by EXPERIENCE HENDRIX, L.L.C.
Copyright Renewed 1995, 1996
All Rights Controlled and Administered by EXPERIENCE HENDRIX, L.L.C.
All Rights Reserved

Additional Lyrics

2. Wait a minute, something's wrong here.
The key won't unlock the door.
Wait a minute, something's wrong.
Lord, have mercy, this key won't unlock this door.
Something's goin' wrong here.
I have a bad, bad feeling
That my baby don't live here no more.
That's alright, I still got my guitar. Look out now!
Yeah! That's alright!

3. Well, I might as well go back over yonder,
Way back among the hills.
Yeah, that's what I'm gonna do.
Lord, I might as well go back over yonder,
Way back yonder 'cross the hills.
'Cause if my baby don't love me no more,
I know her sister will!
Yeah!

**CD TRACK**
6 Full Stereo Mix
14 Split Mix
C Version

# Spanish Castle Magic

Words and Music by
Jimi Hendrix

Copyright © 1968 by EXPERIENCE HENDRIX, L.L.C.
Copyright Renewed 1996
All Rights Controlled and Administered by EXPERIENCE HENDRIX, L.L.C.
All Rights Reserved

Additional Lyrics

2. The clouds are really low, and they overflow with cotton candy
And battlegrounds, red and brown.
But it's all in your mind, don't think your time on bad things.
Just float your little mind around. Look out! Ooh! Heh.

Hang on my darlin', yeah. Hang on if you wanna go.
It's a, hah, look at you girl, you make me laugh, it's a,
Just a little bit of Spanish castle magic.
Yeah baby, it's a, uh hah.

D.S. Hang on my darlin'. Hey. Hang on, hang on if you wanna go.
It's a, oh girl, heh, that's right baby. It's a,
A little bit of Spanish castle magic.
Hey. Little bit of Spanish castle magic.

CD TRACK

7 Full Stereo Mix

15 Split Mix

C Version

# Voodoo Child (Slight Return)

Words and Music by
Jimi Hendrix

Copyright © 1968, 1980 by EXPERIENCE HENDRIX, L.L.C.
Copyright Renewed 1996
All Rights Controlled and Administered by EXPERIENCE HENDRIX, L.L.C.
All Rights Reserved

Verse
E
2. I did-n't mean _ to _ take up all your _ sweet time.
I'll give it right back to you a one of these _ days. _ Ha, ha, ha.
I said I did-n't mean to take up all your sweet time, _ I'll give it right back _ one of these
days. Yeah. If I don't meet you no more in this world, _ then uh,
E7(omit3)/D
A/C♯
E
E7
I'll meet you on the next one, and don't be late. _ Don't be late. 'Cause I'm a
C7
D7
voo-doo child, _ voo-doo child, _ Lord _ knows _ I'm a voo-doo _ child. _ Hey,
Outro/Guitar Solo
hey, hey. I'm a voo-doo child, ba-by.
I don't take _ no _ for an an - swer. _
ques - tion no. _

**CD TRACK**

8 Full Stereo Mix

16 Split Mix

C Version

# Who Knows

Words and Music by
Jimi Hendrix

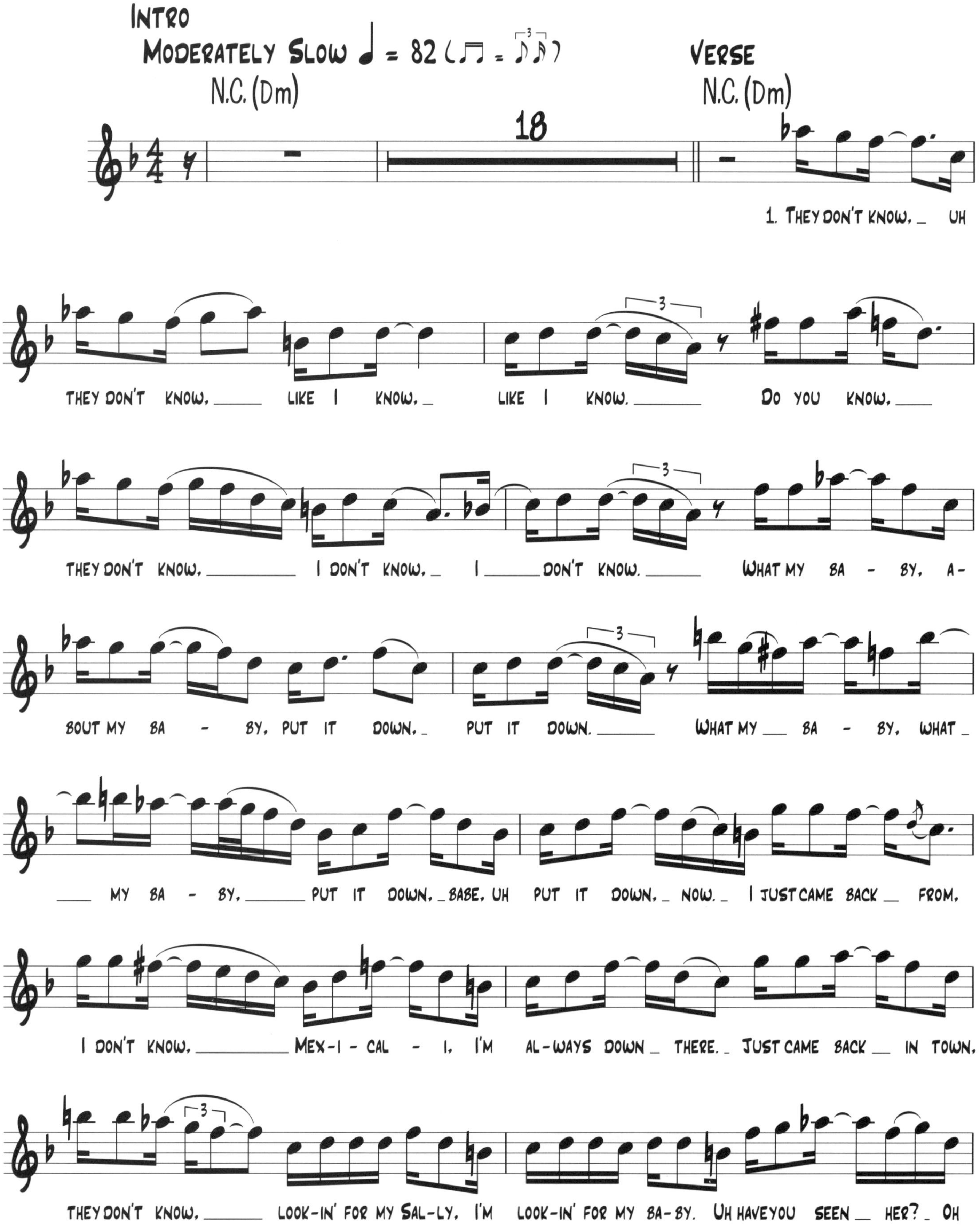

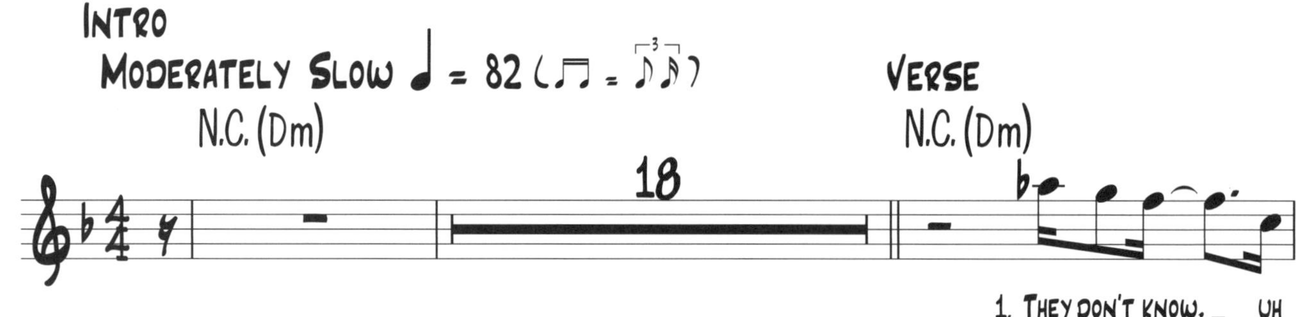

Intro
Moderately Slow ♩ = 82 (♫ = ♪♪ triplet)
N.C.(Dm)
18
Verse
N.C.(Dm)
1. They don't know, _ uh
they don't know, _ like I know, _ like I know. _ Do you know, _
they don't know, _ I don't know, _ I _ don't know. _ What my ba - by, a-
bout my ba - by, put it down, _ put it down. _ What my _ ba - by, what _
_ my ba - by, _ put it down, _ babe, uh put it down, _ now. _ I just came back _ from,
I don't know, _ Mex - i - cal - i, I'm al - ways down _ there. _ Just came back _ in town,
they don't know, _ look-in' for my Sal-ly, I'm look-in' for my ba - by. Uh have you seen _ her? _ Oh

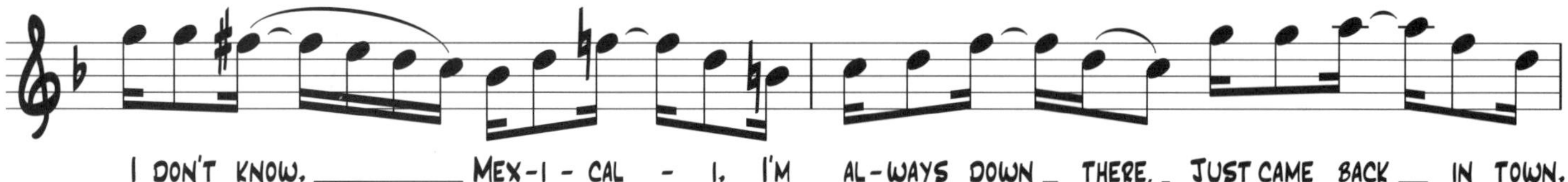

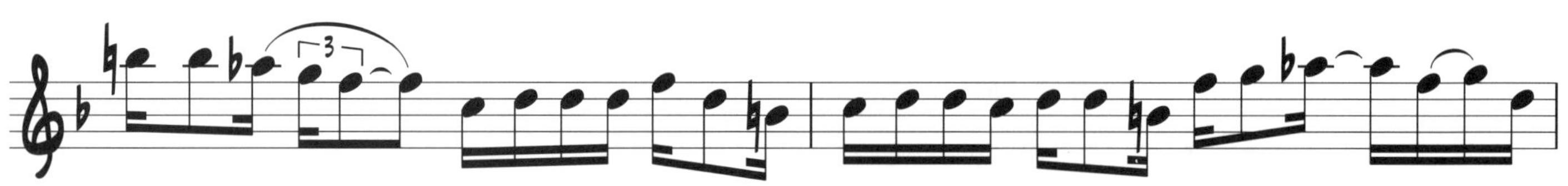

Copyright © 1970 by EXPERIENCE HENDRIX, L.L.C.
Copyright Renewed 1998
All Rights Controlled and Administered by EXPERIENCE HENDRIX, L.L.C.
All Rights Reserved

I BE FREE. YEAH. OH HAVE YOU SEEN HER? OOH HOO. TALK-IN' 'BOUT MY.
GUITAR SOLO
N.C. (Dm)
11
GO-IN' DOWN. TALK-IN' A-BOUT MY BA-BY.
VERSE
N.C. (Dm)
2. JUST CAME IN. JUST CAME IN. BABE. JUST CAME IN.
CAME IN. SPREAD-IN' MAG - IC HON-EY ALL IN MY BED.
SHE GOT CHAINS AT-TACHED TO MY HEAD. TALK-IN' A-BOUT.
3
TALK-IN' A-BOUT. TALK-IN' A-BOUT MY BA - BY. UH I DON'T KNOW 'BOUT.
GUITAR SOLO
N.C. (Dm)
26
VOCAL SOLO
N.C. (Dm)
OUTRO
N.C. (Dm)
PLAY 4 TIMES
4

CD TRACK

1 Full Stereo Mix

9 Split Mix

B♭ Version

# Fire

Words and Music by
Jimi Hendrix

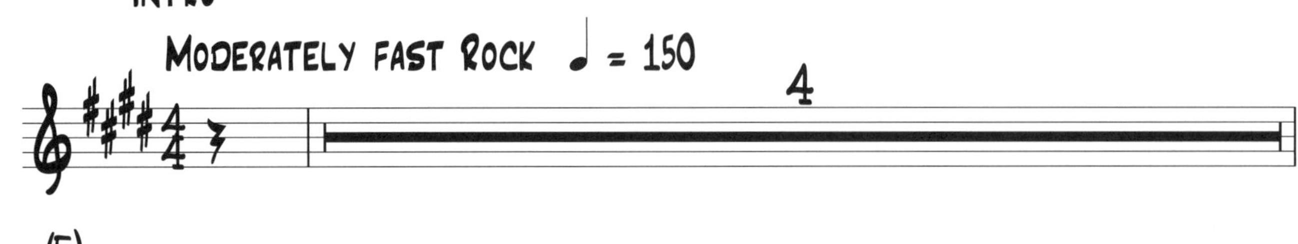

Copyright © 1967, 1968, 1980 by EXPERIENCE HENDRIX, L.L.C.
Copyright Renewed 1995, 1996
All Rights Controlled and Administered by EXPERIENCE HENDRIX, L.L.C.
All Rights Reserved

To Coda
Eadd9
Dadd9
Eadd9
Dadd9
BA - BY!
LET ME STAND _ NEXT TO YOUR FIRE! _
LET ME STAND. ___
LET ME STAND _ NEXT TO YOUR
YEAH, _ BA - BY!
FIRE!) _
1.
N.C. (E)
LIS-TEN HERE, BA - BY,
AND STOP ACT-ING SO CRA-ZY.
2. YOU SAY YOUR
2.
BRIDGE
E
OH! __ MOVE O - VER, _
___ ROV - ER, __
Dadd9
AND LET JIM - I TAKE O - VER!
B
YEAH, YOU KNOW WHAT I'M TALK-ING _ 'BOUT!
D
8VA
YEAH! _
LOCO
GET ON WITH IT, BA - BY!
GUITAR SOLO
N.C. (F#)
8
INTERLUDE
N.C.
THAT'S WHAT I'M TALK-ING 'BOUT. _
NOW, DIG THIS!
(E)
HA!
NOW LIS-TEN, BA-BY!
D.S. AL CODA
3. YOU TRY TO

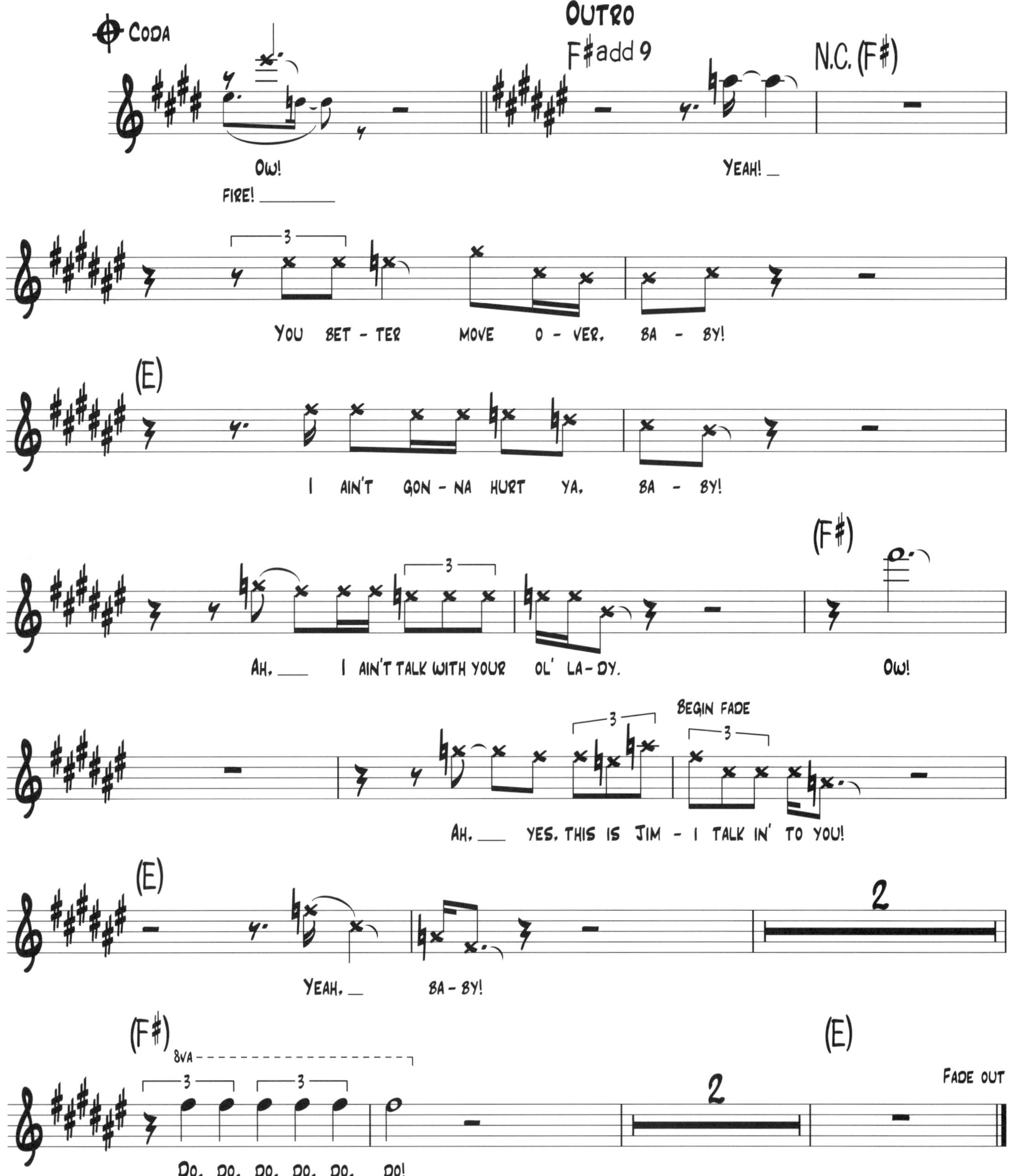


### ADDITIONAL LYRICS

2. YOU SAY YOUR MUM AIN'T HOME, IT AIN'T MY CONCERN.
   JUST A PLAY WITH ME, AND YOU WON'T GET BURNED.
   I HAVE ONLY ONE A ITCHING DESIRE,
   LET ME STAND NEXT TO YOUR FIRE!

3. YOU TRY TO GIMME YOUR MONEY, YOU BETTER SAVE IT BABE,
   SAVE IT FOR YOUR RAINY DAY.
   I HAVE ONLY ONE A BURNING DESIRE,
   LET ME STAND NEXT TO YOUR FIRE!

**CD TRACK**

2 FULL STEREO MIX

10 SPLIT MIX

$B^{\flat}$ VERSION

# FOXEY LADY

WORDS AND MUSIC BY
JIMI HENDRIX

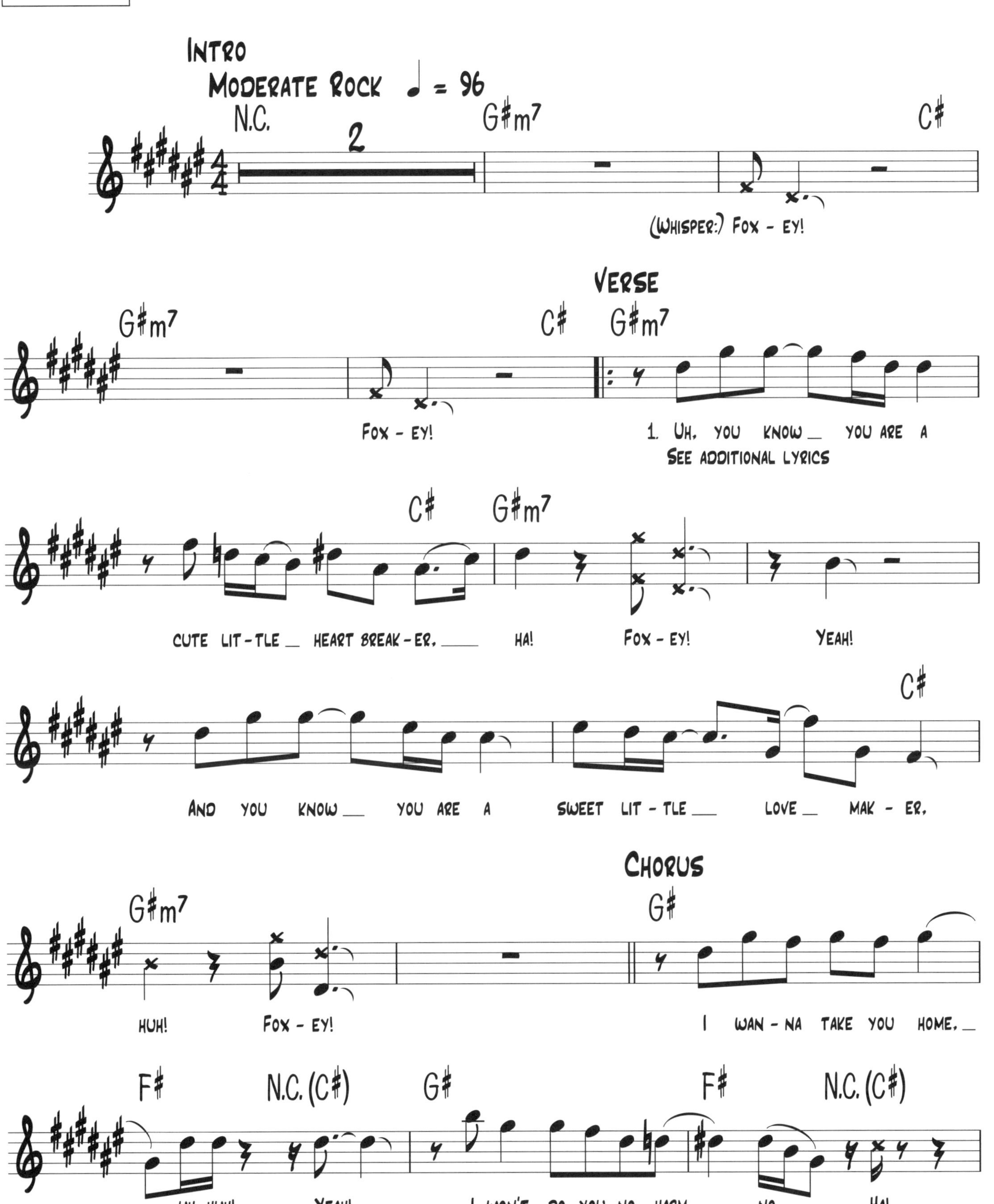


COPYRIGHT © 1967, 1968, 1980 BY EXPERIENCE HENDRIX, L.L.C.
COPYRIGHT RENEWED 1995, 1996
ALL RIGHTS CONTROLLED AND ADMINISTERED BY EXPERIENCE HENDRIX, L.L.C.
ALL RIGHTS RESERVED

G#m7
F#
N.C. (C#)
G#
N.C.
YOU'VE GOT TO BE ALL MINE, ALL MINE.
OOH! FOX-EY LA-DY!
1.
G#m7
G#7#9
N.C.
G#m7
YEAH!
(WHISPER:) FOX-EY!
C#
2.
GUITAR SOLO
G#m7
FOX-EY! 2. NOW A
HERE I COME!
FOX-EY LA-DY!
FOX-EY LA-DY!
FOX-EY! FOX-EY!
FOX-EY! YEAH!
CHORUS
G#
5
F#
N.C. (C#)
G#
I'M GON-NA TAKE YOU HOME, UH, HUH!
I WON'T DO YOU NO HARM,
F#
N.C. (C#)
G#
F#
N.C. (C#)
NO.
YOU'VE GOT TO BE ALL MINE, ALL MINE.
FREE TIME
G#
N.C.
3
FOX-EY LA-DY!
HERE I COME, BA-BY.
I'M COM-IN' TO GET YA!

### Additional Lyrics

2. Now I see you, come on down on the scene. Oh foxey.
You make me wanna get up and scream! Foxey!
Oh, baby listen now.

Chorus I've made up my mind.
I'm tired of wasting all my precious time.
You've got to be all mine, all mine.
Foxey lady!
Here I come!

CD TRACK

3 Full Stereo Mix

11 Split Mix

B♭ Version

# JAM 292

Words and Music by
Jimi Hendrix

Intro
Moderate Shuffle ♩. = 106

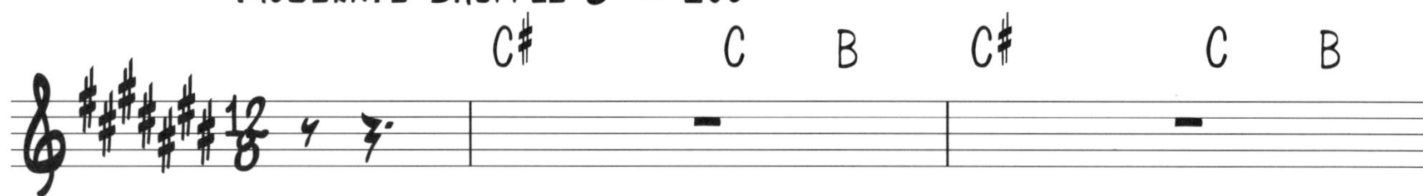


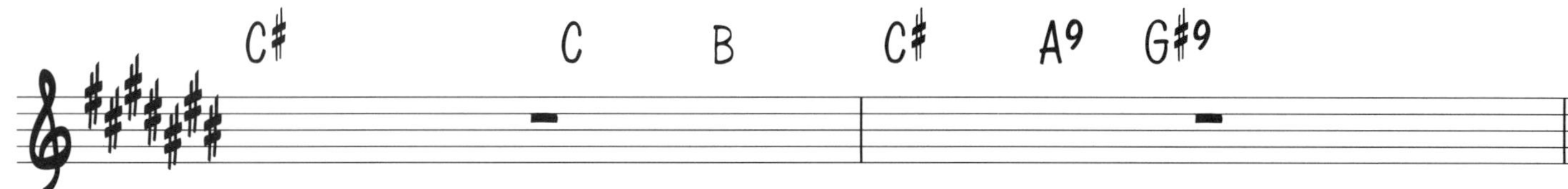


Riff 1/Guitar Solo (2nd/3rd times)

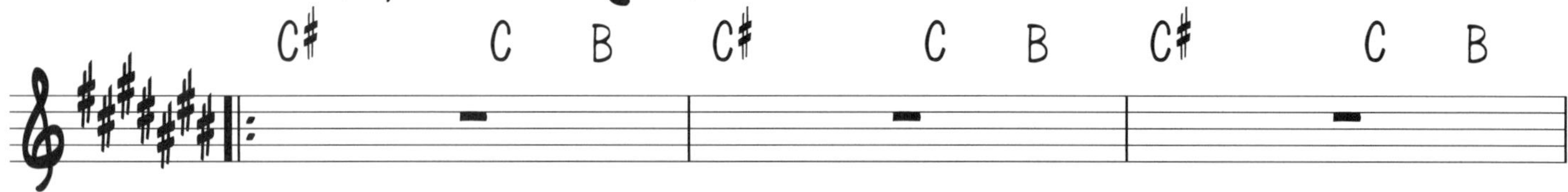


C# C B F# F E F# F E

C# C B C# C B G# G F#

Riff 2

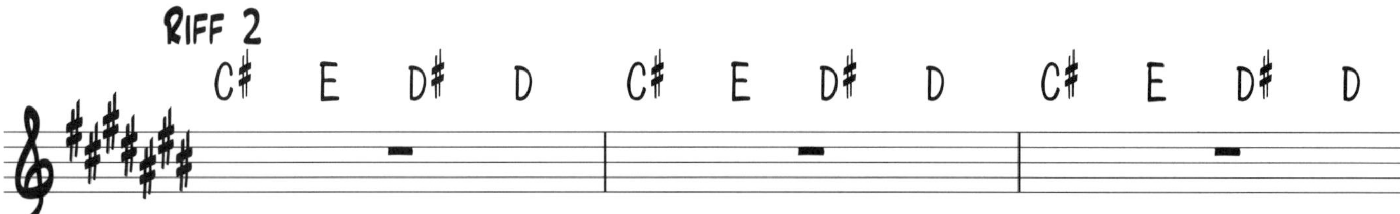


Copyright © 1973 by EXPERIENCE HENDRIX, L.L.C.
Copyright Renewed 2001
All Rights Controlled and Administered by EXPERIENCE HENDRIX, L.L.C.
All Rights Reserved

C♯ E D♯ D F♯ A G♯ G F♯ A G♯ G
C♯ E D♯ D C♯ E D♯ D G♯ B A♯ A
F♯ A G♯ G C♯ E D♯ D C♯ E D♯ D
Riff 3
C♯7
3
F♯7
C♯7
G♯7
F♯7
C♯7
Riff 4
C♯7
3
F♯7
C♯7
G♯7
F♯7
C♯7
Play 3 times
Guitar Solo 2/Riff 4
C♯7
3
F♯7
C♯7
G♯7
F♯7
C♯7
Outro
C♯7
2
Play 3 times

**CD TRACK**

4 Full Stereo Mix

12 Split Mix

B♭ Version

# Little Wing

Words and Music by
Jimi Hendrix

Copyright © 1968 by EXPERIENCE HENDRIX, L.L.C.
Copyright Renewed 1996
All Rights Controlled and Administered by EXPERIENCE HENDRIX, L.L.C.
All Rights Reserved

A
Bm
F#m
WITH A THOU - SAND SMILES _ SHE GIVES TO ME ____ FREE. _
C#m
C
Bm
D
IT'S AL - RIGHT, SHE ___ SAID, _ IT'S AL-RIGHT, TAKE __ AN - Y - THING __ YOU WANT _
A
Gadd9
D
___ FROM ME. __________ AN - Y - THING. _
GUITAR SOLO
E
F#m
AN - Y - THING. __________
A
Bm
F#m
FLY ON. __ LIT-TLE WING. ______
C#m C Bm D A Gadd9 D E
OUTRO
F#m
A
Bm
F#m
YEAH, YEAH, YEAH, ________ LIT-TLE WING. ______
C#m C Bm D A Gadd9 D E

Copyright © 1967, 1968, 1980 by EXPERIENCE HENDRIX, L.L.C.
Copyright Renewed 1995, 1996
All Rights Controlled and Administered by EXPERIENCE HENDRIX, L.L.C.
All Rights Reserved

ADDITIONAL LYRICS

2. WAIT A MINUTE, SOMETHING'S WRONG HERE,
THE KEY WON'T UNLOCK THE DOOR.
WAIT A MINUTE, SOMETHING'S WRONG,
LORD, HAVE MERCY, THIS KEY WON'T UNLOCK THIS DOOR.
SOMETHING'S GOIN' WRONG HERE.
I HAVE A BAD, BAD FEELING
THAT MY BABY DON'T LIVE HERE NO MORE.
THAT'S ALRIGHT, I STILL GOT MY GUITAR. LOOK OUT NOW!
YEAH! THAT'S ALRIGHT!

3. WELL, I MIGHT AS WELL GO BACK OVER YONDER,
WAY BACK AMONG THE HILLS.
YEAH, THAT'S WHAT I'M GONNA DO.
LORD, I MIGHT AS WELL GO BACK OVER YONDER,
WAY BACK YONDER 'CROSS THE HILLS.
'CAUSE IF MY BABY DON'T LOVE ME NO MORE,
I KNOW HER SISTER WILL!
YEAH!

**CD TRACK**

6 Full Stereo Mix

14 Split Mix

B♭ Version

# Spanish Castle Magic

Words and Music by
Jimi Hendrix

Copyright © 1968 by EXPERIENCE HENDRIX, L.L.C.
Copyright Renewed 1996
All Rights Controlled and Administered by EXPERIENCE HENDRIX, L.L.C.
All Rights Reserved

Additional Lyrics

2. The clouds are really low, and they overflow with cotton candy
and battlegrounds, red and brown.
But it's all in your mind, don't think your time on bad things.
Just float your little mind around. Look out! Ooh! Heh.

Hang on my darlin', yeah. Hang on if you wanna go.
It's a, hah, look at you girl, you make me laugh, it's a,
Just a little bit of Spanish castle magic.
Yeah baby, it's a, uh hah.

D.S. Hang on my darlin'. Hey. Hang on, hang on if you wanna go.
It's a, oh girl, heh, that's right baby. It's a,
A little bit of Spanish castle magic.
Hey. Little bit of Spanish castle magic.

CD TRACK
7 Full Stereo Mix
15 Split Mix
B♭ Version

# Voodoo Child (Slight Return)

Words and Music by
Jimi Hendrix

Copyright © 1968, 1980 by EXPERIENCE HENDRIX, L.L.C.
Copyright Renewed 1996
All Rights Controlled and Administered by EXPERIENCE HENDRIX, L.L.C.
All Rights Reserved

Verse
F♯
2
2. I did-n't mean _ to _ take up all your _ sweet time.
I'll give it right back to you a one of these _ days. _ Ha, ha, ha.
2
I said I did-n't mean to take up all your sweet time. _ I'll give it right back _ one of these
days. Yeah. If I don't meet you no more in this world, _ then uh,
F♯7(omit3)/E
B/D♯
F♯
F♯7
I'll meet you on the next one, and don't be late. _ Don't be late. 'Cause I'm a
D7
E7
F♯
voo-doo child, _ voo-doo child, _ Lord _ knows _ I'm a voo-doo _ child. _ Hey.
Outro/Guitar Solo
F♯
Hey, hey. I'm a voo-doo child, ba-by.
I don't take _ no _ for an an - swer. _
Ques - tion no. _
2

CD TRACK

8 Full Stereo Mix

16 Split Mix

B♭ Version

# Who Knows

Words and Music by
Jimi Hendrix

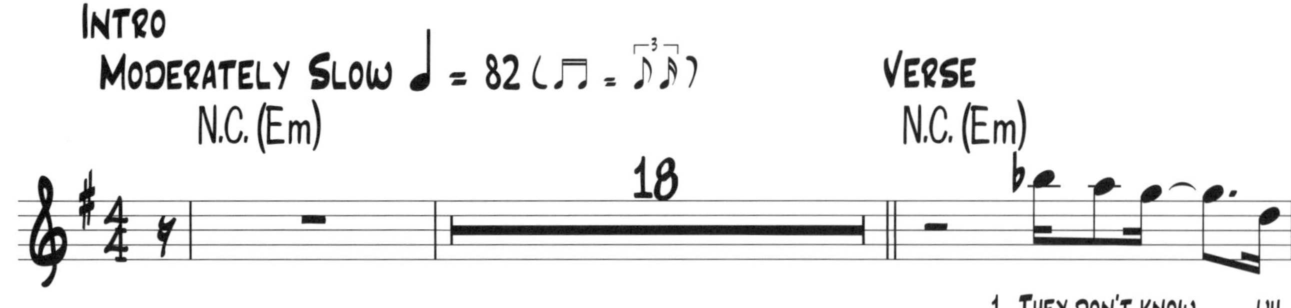

Copyright © 1970 by EXPERIENCE HENDRIX, L.L.C.
Copyright Renewed 1998
All Rights Controlled and Administered by EXPERIENCE HENDRIX, L.L.C.
All Rights Reserved

I BE FREE, YEAH. OH HAVE YOU SEEN HER? OOH HOO. TALK-IN' 'BOUT MY,
GUITAR SOLO
N.C. (Em)
11
GO-IN' DOWN, TALK-IN' A-BOUT MY BA-BY.
VERSE
N.C. (Em)
2. JUST CAME IN, JUST CAME IN, BABE. JUST CAME IN,
CAME IN. SPREAD-IN' MAG - IC HON-EY ALL IN MY BED.
SHE GOT CHAINS AT-TACHED TO MY HEAD. TALK-IN' A-BOUT,
3
TALK-IN' A-BOUT, TALK-IN' A-BOUT MY BA - BY. UH I DON'T KNOW 'BOUT.
GUITAR SOLO
N.C. (Em)
26
VOCAL SOLO
N.C. (Em)
OUTRO
N.C. (Em)
PLAY 4 TIMES
4

**CD TRACK**

1 Full Stereo Mix

9 Split Mix

E♭ Version

# Fire

Words and Music by
Jimi Hendrix

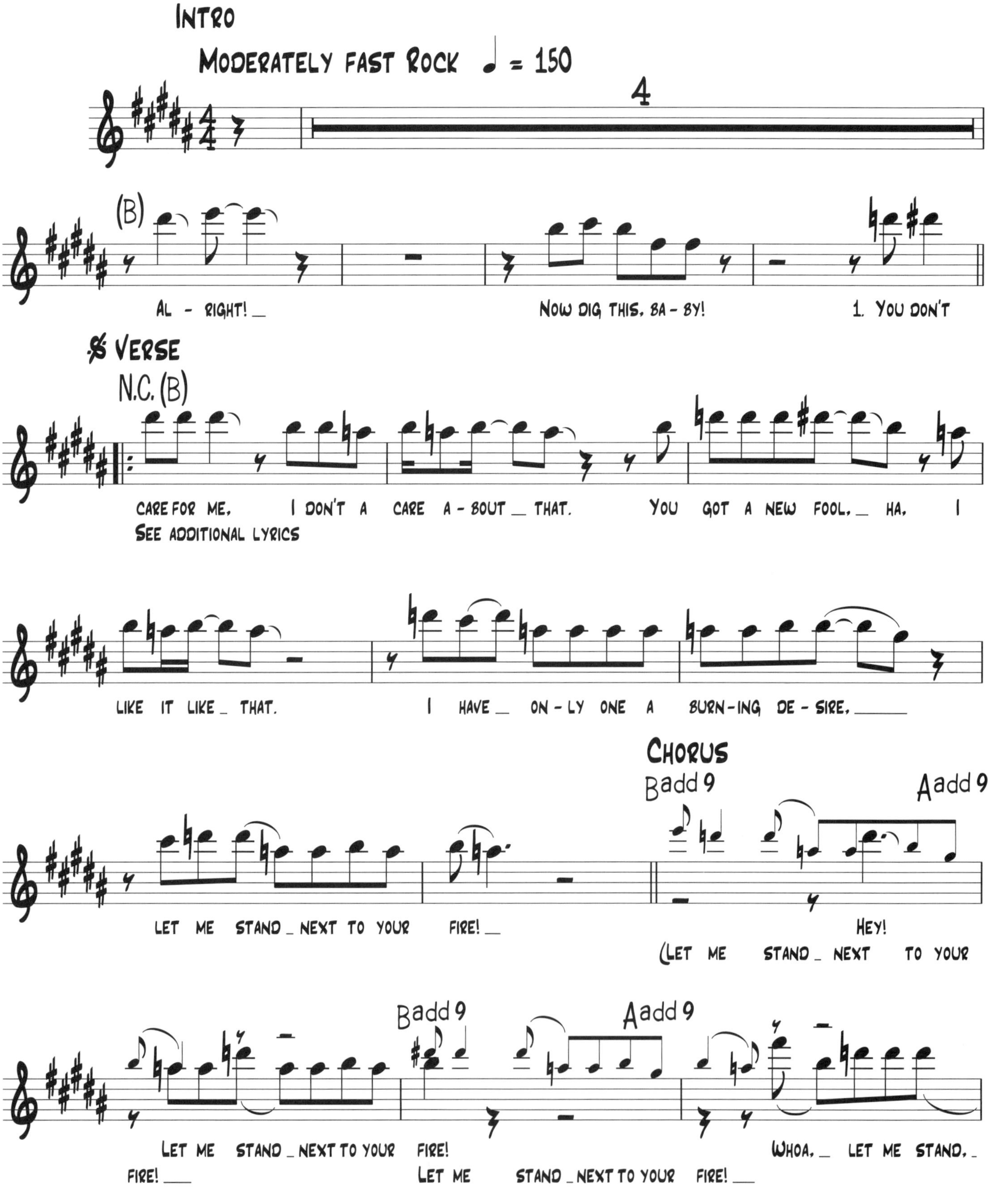

Intro

Moderately fast Rock ♩ = 150

4

(B)

Al - right! _ Now dig this, ba - by! 1. You don't

𝄋 Verse

N.C.(B)

care for me, I don't a care a - bout _ that. You got a new fool, _ ha, I

See additional lyrics

like it like _ that. I have _ on - ly one a burn - ing de - sire, _____

Chorus

Badd9 Aadd9

let me stand _ next to your fire! _ Hey!

(Let me stand _ next to your

Badd9 Aadd9

Let me stand _ next to your fire! Whoa, _ let me stand, _

fire! ___ Let me stand _ next to your fire! ___

Copyright © 1967, 1968, 1980 by EXPERIENCE HENDRIX, L.L.C.
Copyright Renewed 1995, 1996
All Rights Controlled and Administered by EXPERIENCE HENDRIX, L.L.C.
All Rights Reserved

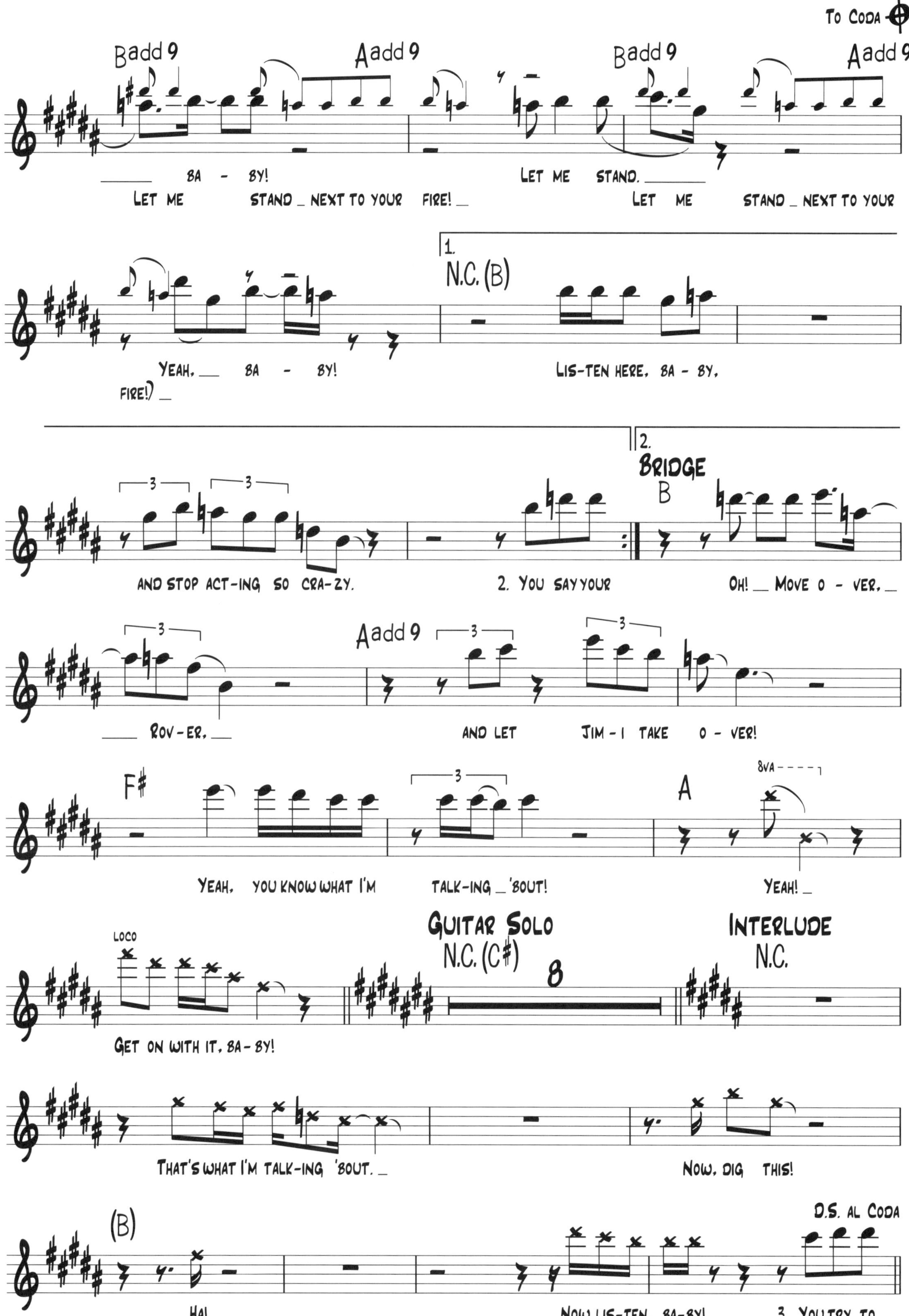
To Coda
Badd9
Aadd9
Badd9
Aadd9
BA - BY!
LET ME STAND.
LET ME STAND _ NEXT TO YOUR FIRE!
LET ME STAND _ NEXT TO YOUR
1.
N.C.(B)
YEAH, BA - BY!
LIS-TEN HERE, BA - BY,
FIRE!)
AND STOP ACT-ING SO CRA-ZY.
2. YOU SAY YOUR
2.
BRIDGE
B
OH! MOVE O - VER,
Aadd9
ROV - ER,
AND LET JIM - I TAKE O - VER!
F#
A
8VA
YEAH, YOU KNOW WHAT I'M TALK-ING 'BOUT!
YEAH!
LOCO
GUITAR SOLO
N.C.(C#)
8
INTERLUDE
N.C.
GET ON WITH IT, BA - BY!
THAT'S WHAT I'M TALK-ING 'BOUT.
NOW, DIG THIS!
(B)
D.S. AL CODA
HA!
NOW LIS-TEN, BA-BY!
3. YOU TRY TO

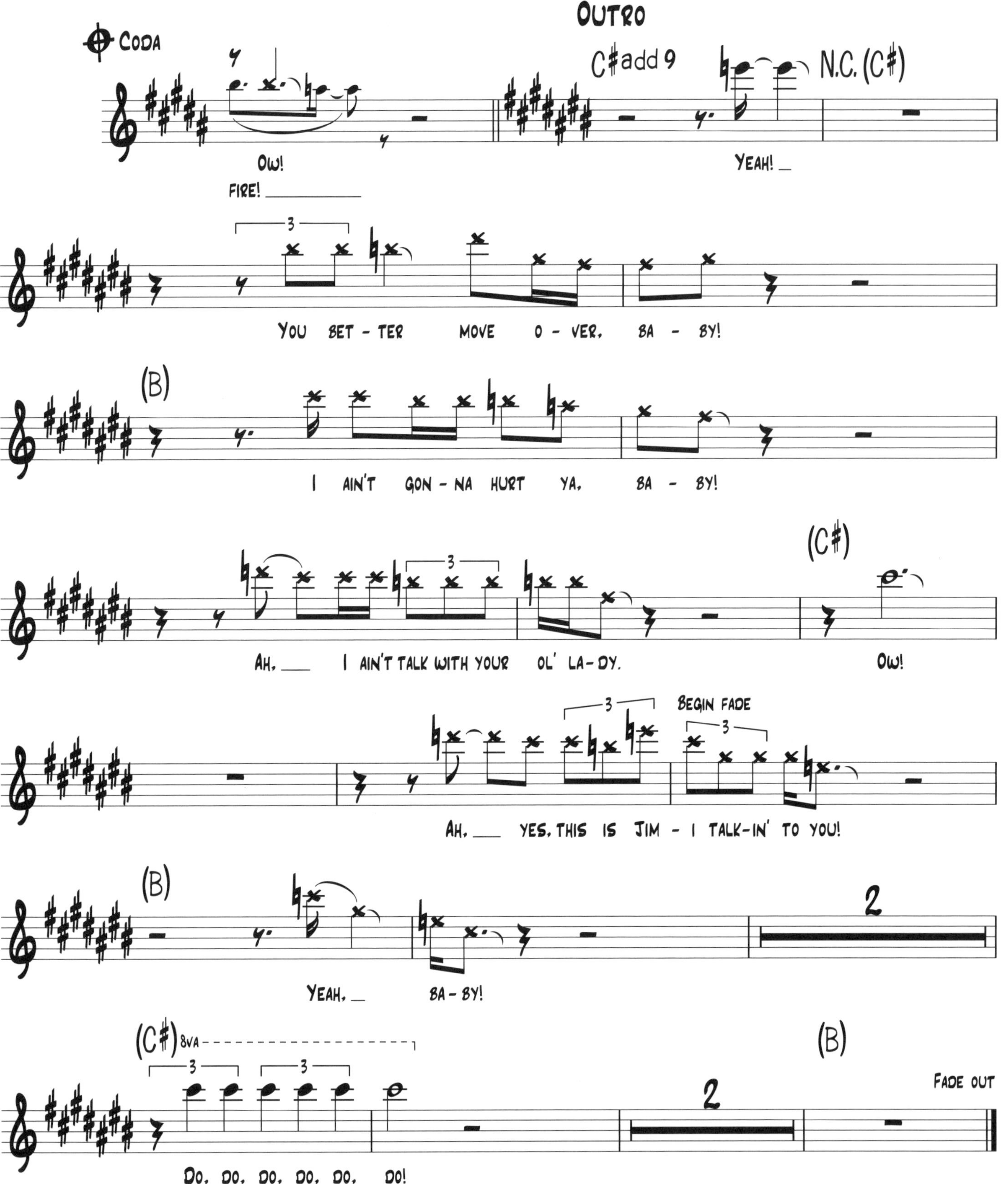


### Additional Lyrics

2. You say your mum ain't home, it ain't my concern.
   Just a play with me, and you won't get burned.
   I have only one a itching desire,
   Let me stand next to your fire!

3. You try to gimme your money, you better save it babe,
   Save it for your rainy day.
   I have only one a burning desire,
   Let me stand next to your fire!

**CD TRACK**

2 Full Stereo Mix

10 Split Mix

E♭ Version

# Foxey Lady

Words and Music by
Jimi Hendrix

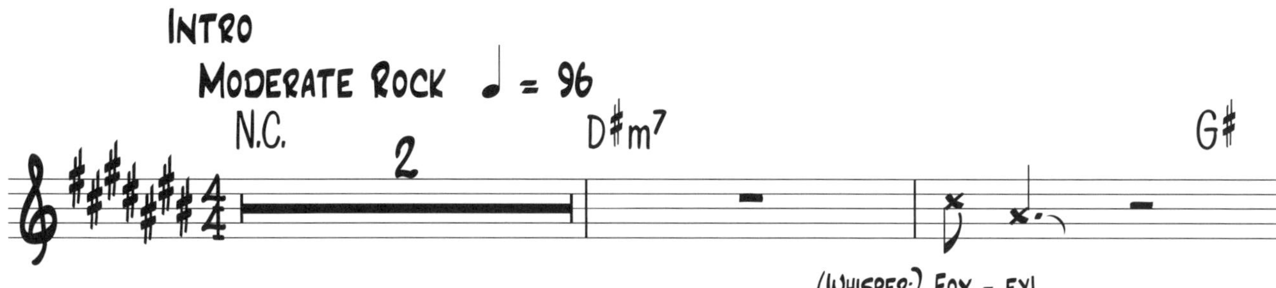

Copyright © 1967, 1968, 1980 by EXPERIENCE HENDRIX, L.L.C.
Copyright Renewed 1995, 1996
All Rights Controlled and Administered by EXPERIENCE HENDRIX, L.L.C.
All Rights Reserved

D♯m7
C♯
N.C. (G♯)
D♯
N.C.
YOU'VE GOT TO BE ALL MINE, ____ ALL _ MINE. _ OOH! FOX-EY LA - DY!
1.
D♯m7
D♯7♯9
N.C.
D♯m7
YEAH! (WHISPER:) FOX - EY!
G♯
2.
GUITAR SOLO
D♯m7
FOX - EY! 2. NOW A HERE I COME! _
FOX - EY LA - DY! FOX - EY LA - DY!
FOX - EY! FOX - EY! FOX - EY! YEAH!
CHORUS
D♯
5
C♯
N.C. (G♯)
D♯
I'M GON-NA TAKE YOU HOME, __ UH, HUH! I WON'T DO YOU NO HARM, _
C♯
N.C. (G♯)
D♯
C♯
N.C. (G♯)
____ NO. ______ YOU'VE GOT TO BE ALL MINE, ALL _ MINE. _
FREE TIME
D♯
N.C.
3
FOX-EY LA - DY! __ HERE I COME, BA-BY. I'M COM IN' TO GET YA!

Additional Lyrics

2. Now I see you, come on down on the scene. Oh foxey.
You make me wanna get up and scream! Foxey!
Oh, baby listen now.

Chorus I've made up my mind.
I'm tired of wasting all my precious time.
You've got to be all mine, all mine.
Foxey lady!
Here I come!

**CD TRACK**

3 Full Stereo Mix

11 Split Mix

E♭ Version

# Jam 292

Words and Music by
Jimi Hendrix

Copyright © 1973 by EXPERIENCE HENDRIX, L.L.C.
Copyright Renewed 2001
All Rights Controlled and Administered by EXPERIENCE HENDRIX, L.L.C.
All Rights Reserved

A♭ C♭ B♭ A D♭ F♭ E♭ D D♭ F♭ E♭ D
A♭ C♭ B♭ A A♭ C♭ B♭ A E♭ G♭ F F♭
D♭ F♭ E♭ D A♭ C♭ B♭ A A♭ C♭ B♭ A
Riff 3
A♭7 3 D♭7 A♭7
E♭7 D♭7 A♭7
Riff 4
A♭7 3 D♭7 A♭7
E♭7 D♭7 A♭7
Play 3 times
Guitar Solo 2/Riff 4
A♭7 3 D♭7 A♭7
E♭7 D♭7 A♭7
Outro
A♭7 2
Play 3 times

**CD TRACK**

4 Full Stereo Mix

12 Split Mix

E♭ Version

# Little Wing

Words and Music by
Jimi Hendrix

Copyright © 1968 by EXPERIENCE HENDRIX, L.L.C.
Copyright Renewed 1996
All Rights Controlled and Administered by EXPERIENCE HENDRIX, L.L.C.
All Rights Reserved

E F#m C#m
WITH A THOU - SAND SMILES SHE GIVES TO ME FREE.
G#m G F#m A
IT'S AL - RIGHT, SHE SAID, IT'S AL-RIGHT, TAKE AN - Y - THING YOU WANT
E Dadd9 A
FROM ME. AN - Y - THING,
GUITAR SOLO
B C#m
AN - Y - THING.
E F#m C#m
FLY ON, LIT-TLE WING.
G#m G F#m A E Dadd9 A B
OUTRO
C#m E F#m C#m
YEAH, YEAH, YEAH, LIT-TLE WING.
G#m G F#m A E Dadd9 A B

Copyright © 1967, 1968, 1980 by EXPERIENCE HENDRIX, L.L.C.
Copyright Renewed 1995, 1996
All Rights Controlled and Administered by EXPERIENCE HENDRIX, L.L.C.
All Rights Reserved

Additional Lyrics

2. Wait a minute, something's wrong here.
The key won't unlock the door.
Wait a minute, something's wrong.
Lord, have mercy, this key won't unlock this door.
Something's goin' wrong here.
I have a bad, bad feeling
That my baby don't live here no more.
That's alright, I still got my guitar. Look out now!
Yeah! That's alright!

3. Well, I might as well go back over yonder,
Way back among the hills.
Yeah, that's what I'm gonna do.
Lord, I might as well go back over yonder,
Way back yonder 'cross the hills.
'Cause if my baby don't love me no more,
I know her sister will!
Yeah!

**CD TRACK**
6 Full Stereo Mix
14 Split Mix
E♭ Version

# Spanish Castle Magic

Words and Music by
Jimi Hendrix

Intro
Moderately ♩ = 98

N.C. C#5 A#5 A#7#9 C#5 A#5 A#7#9

Verse

G#5 G5 B5/F#

1. It's ver - y far a - way, __ it takes a-bout a half a day to
2. See additional lyrics

A#5/F A# G#5

get there if we trav-el by my, uh, drag-on - fly. No it's not in __ Spain, _

G5 B5/F# A#5/F

but all the same, you know it's a, a groov y name, _ and the wind's _ just _

Chorus

A#7 F#5 D#5 D#m7 F#5 D#5 D#m7

____ right. hey. ow. Hang __ on __ my dar - lin'.
D.S. See additional Lyrics

C#5 A#5 A#7#9 C#5 A#5 A#7#9

hang on ______ if you wan - na go. __________________ You

E#m7 C#

know it's a real - ly groov - y place, _ it's a, heh, uh just a lit - tle bit of, said uh,

Copyright © 1968 by EXPERIENCE HENDRIX, L.L.C.
Copyright Renewed 1996
All Rights Controlled and Administered by EXPERIENCE HENDRIX, L.L.C.
All Rights Reserved

Additional Lyrics

2. The clouds are really low, and they overflow with cotton candy
And battlegrounds, red and brown.
But it's all in your mind, don't think your time on bad things.
Just float your little mind around. Look out! Ooh! Heh.

Hang on my darlin', yeah. Hang on if you wanna go.
It's a, hah, look at you girl, you make me laugh, it's a,
Just a little bit of Spanish castle magic.
Yeah baby, it's a, uh hah.

D.S. Hang on my darlin'. Hey. Hang on, hang on if you wanna go.
It's a, oh girl, heh, that's right baby. It's a,
A little bit of Spanish castle magic.
Hey, little bit of Spanish castle magic.

**CD TRACK**

7 Full Stereo Mix

15 Split Mix

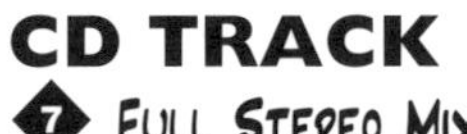

E♭ Version

# Voodoo Child
## (Slight Return)

Words and Music by
Jimi Hendrix

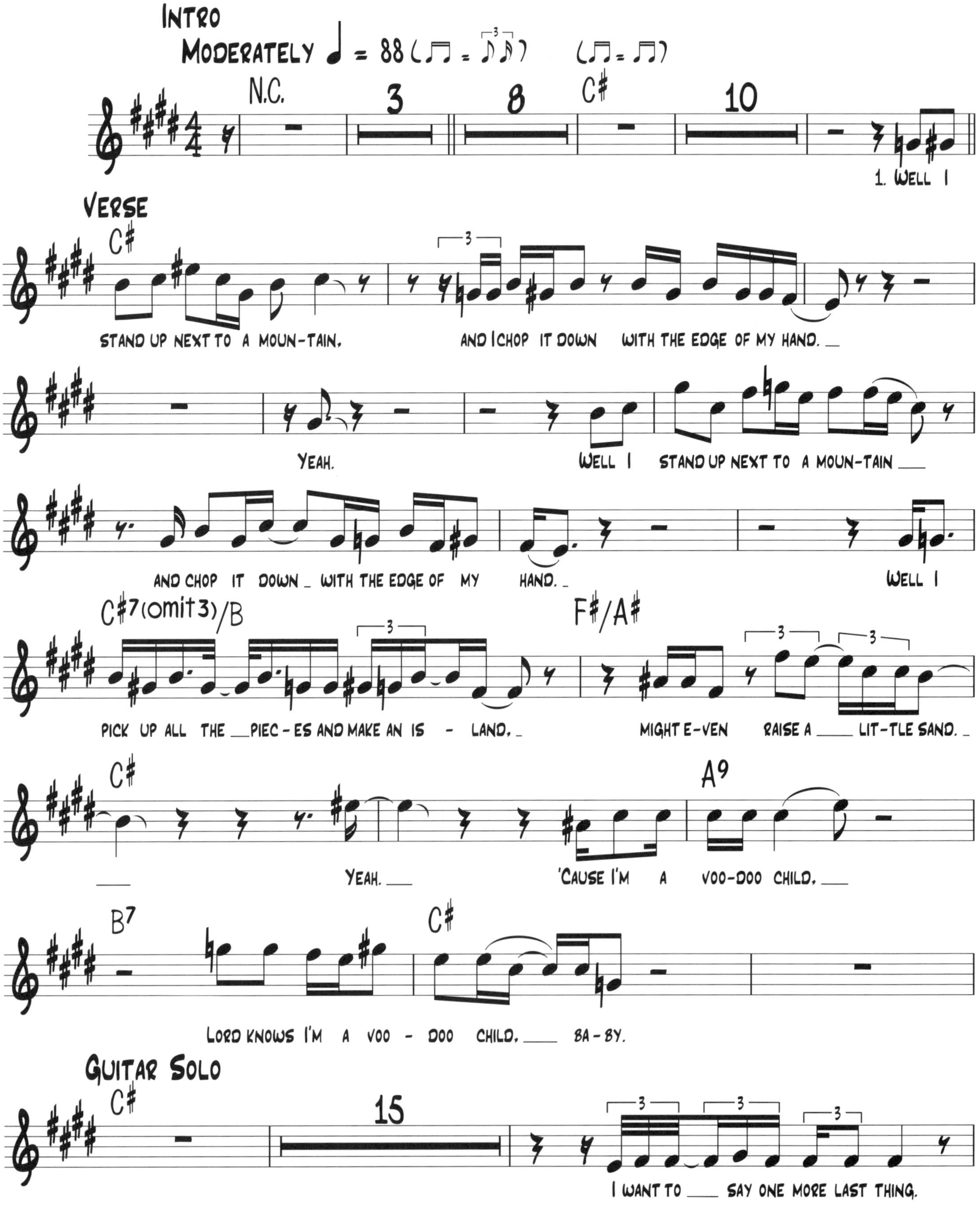

Intro
Moderately ♩ = 88
N.C.
3
8
C♯
10
1. Well I
Verse
C♯
stand up next to a moun-tain, and I chop it down with the edge of my hand.
Yeah.
Well I stand up next to a moun-tain
and chop it down with the edge of my hand.
Well I
C♯7(omit3)/B
F♯/A♯
pick up all the piec-es and make an is - land,
might e-ven raise a lit-tle sand.
C♯
A9
Yeah.
'Cause I'm a voo-doo child,
B7
C♯
Lord knows I'm a voo - doo child, ba-by.
Guitar Solo
C♯
15
I want to say one more last thing.


Copyright © 1968, 1980 by EXPERIENCE HENDRIX, L.L.C.
Copyright Renewed 1996
All Rights Controlled and Administered by EXPERIENCE HENDRIX, L.L.C.
All Rights Reserved

Verse
2
C♯
2. I did-n't mean __ to __ take up all your _ sweet time.
I'll give it right back to you a one of these _ days. _ Ha, ha, ha.
2
I said I did-n't mean to take up all your sweet time. _ I'll give it right back _ one of these
days. Yeah.
C♯7(omit3)/B
If I don't meet you no more in this world, __ then uh,
F♯/A♯
C♯
C♯7
I'll meet you on the next one, and don't be late. _ Don't be late. 'Cause I'm a
A7
B7
C♯
voo-doo child, _ voo-doo child, __ Lord _ knows _ I'm a voo-doo __ child. _ Hey,
Outro/Guitar Solo
C♯
hey, hey. I'm a voo-doo child, ba-by.
I don't take _ no __ for an an - swer. _
question no. __
2

CD TRACK
8 Full Stereo Mix
16 Split Mix
E♭ Version

# Who Knows

Words and Music by
Jimi Hendrix

Copyright © 1970 by EXPERIENCE HENDRIX, L.L.C.
Copyright Renewed 1998
All Rights Controlled and Administered by EXPERIENCE HENDRIX, L.L.C.
All Rights Reserved

I be free, yeah. Oh have you seen her? Ooh hoo. Talk-in' 'bout my.
Guitar Solo
N.C. (Bm)
11
go-in' down, talk-in' a-bout my ba-by.
Verse
N.C. (Bm)
2. Just came in, just came in, babe. Just came in,
came in. Spread-in' mag - ic hon-ey all in my bed.
She got chains at-tached to my head. Talk-in' a-bout,
3
talk-in' a-bout, talk-in' a-bout my ba - by. Uh I don't know 'bout.
Guitar Solo
N.C. (Bm)
26
Vocal Solo
N.C. (Bm)
Outro
N.C. (Bm)
Play 4 times
4

**CD TRACK**

1 Full Stereo Mix

9 Split Mix

C Version

# Fire

Words and Music by
Jimi Hendrix

Copyright © 1967, 1968, 1980 by EXPERIENCE HENDRIX, L.L.C.
Copyright Renewed 1995, 1996
All Rights Controlled and Administered by EXPERIENCE HENDRIX, L.L.C.
All Rights Reserved

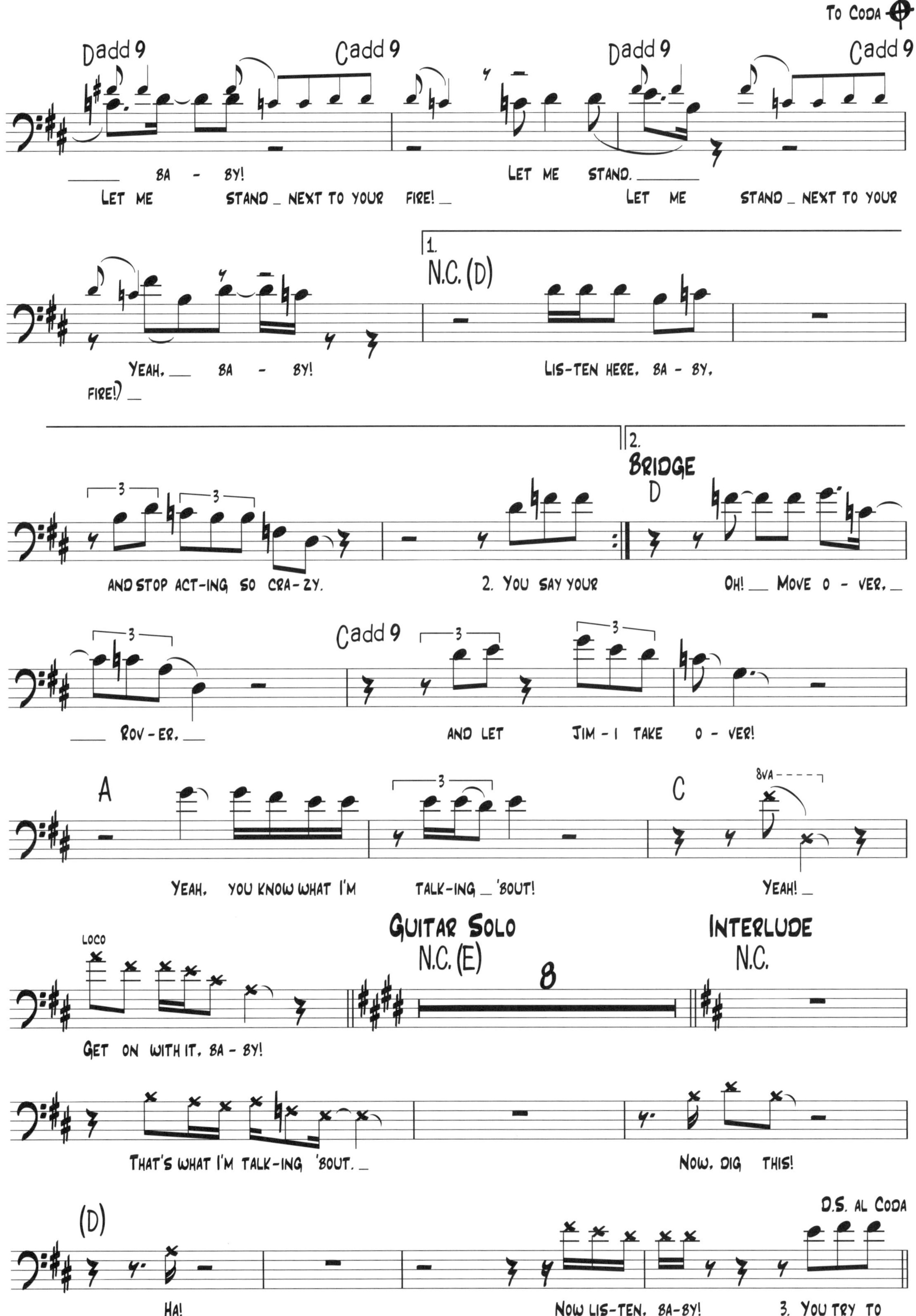
To Coda
Dadd9
Cadd9
Dadd9
Cadd9
ba - by!
Let me stand.
Let me stand _ next to your fire! _
Let me stand _ next to your
1.
N.C.(D)
Yeah, _ ba - by!
fire!) _
Lis-ten here, ba - by,
and stop act-ing so cra-zy.
2. You say your
2.
Bridge
D
Oh! _ Move o - ver, _
Cadd9
_ Rov - er, _
and let Jim - i take o - ver!
A
C
8va
Yeah, you know what I'm talk-ing _ 'bout!
Yeah! _
loco
Guitar Solo
N.C.(E)
8
Interlude
N.C.
Get on with it, ba - by!
That's what I'm talk-ing 'bout. _
Now, dig this!
(D)
D.S. al Coda
Ha!
Now lis-ten, ba-by!
3. You try to

Additional Lyrics

2. You say your mum ain't home, it ain't my concern.
Just a play with me, and you won't get burned.
I have only one a itching desire,
Let me stand next to your fire!

3. You try to gimme your money, you better save it babe,
Save it for your rainy day.
I have only one a burning desire,
Let me stand next to your fire!

CD TRACK

2 Full Stereo Mix

10 Split Mix

𝄢 C Version

# Foxey Lady

Words and Music by
Jimi Hendrix

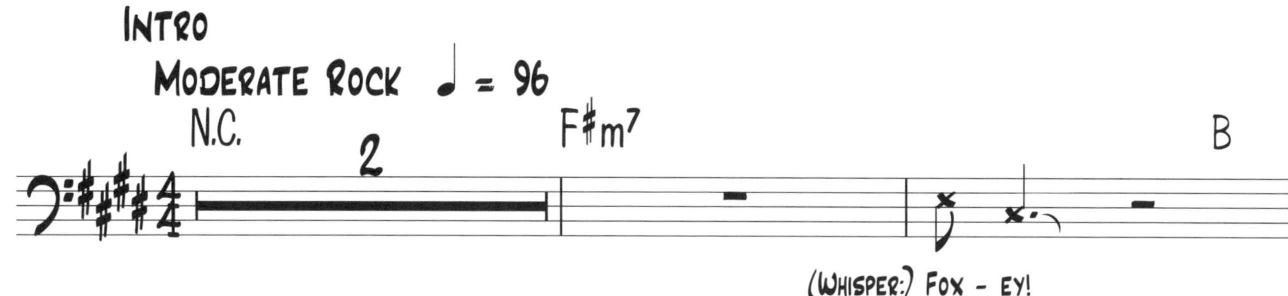


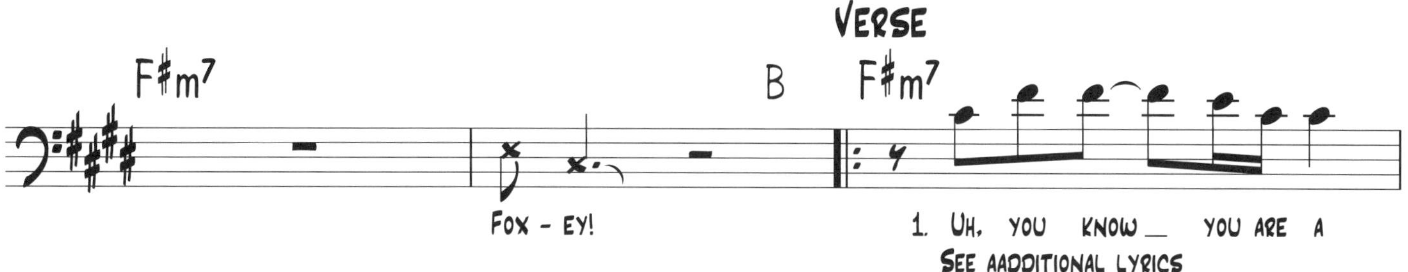

Copyright © 1967, 1968, 1980 by EXPERIENCE HENDRIX, L.L.C.
Copyright Renewed 1995, 1996
All Rights Controlled and Administered by EXPERIENCE HENDRIX, L.L.C.
All Rights Reserved

F#m7
E
N.C. (B)
F#
N.C.
YOU'VE GOT TO BE ALL MINE, ALL MINE. OOH! FOX-EY LA-DY!
1.
F#m7
F#7#9
N.C.
F#m7
YEAH! (WHISPER:) FOX-EY!
B
2.
GUITAR SOLO
F#m7
FOX-EY! 2. NOW A HERE I COME!
FOX-EY LA-DY! FOX-EY LA-DY!
FOX-EY! FOX-EY! FOX-EY! YEAH!
CHORUS
F#
5
E
N.C. (B)
F#
I'M GON-NA TAKE YOU HOME, UH, HUH! I WON'T DO YOU NO HARM,
E
N.C. (B)
F#
E
N.C. (B)
NO. YOU'VE GOT TO BE ALL MINE, ALL MINE.
FREE TIME
F#
N.C.
3
FOX-EY LA-DY! HERE I COME, BA-BY. I'M COM-IN' TO GET YA!

Additional Lyrics

2. Now I see you, come on down on the scene. Oh foxey.
You make me wanna get up and scream! Foxey!
Oh, baby listen now.

Chorus I've made up my mind.
I'm tired of wasting all my precious time.
You've got to be all mine, all mine.
Foxey lady!
Here I come!

**CD TRACK**

3 Full Stereo Mix

11 Split Mix

C Version

# JAM 292

Words and Music by
Jimi Hendrix

Intro
Moderate Shuffle ♩. = 106

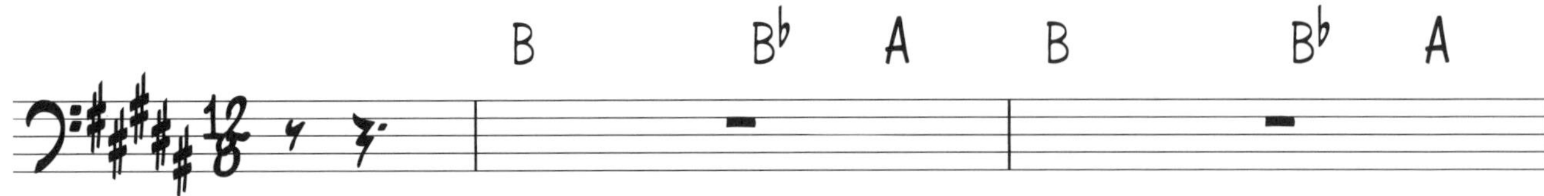

Riff 1/Guitar Solo (2nd/3rd times)

B B♭ A | B B♭ A | B B♭ A

B B♭ A | E E♭ D | E E♭ D

B B♭ A | B B♭ A | F♯ F E

E♭ D | B B♭ A | B B♭ A

End Solo 3rd time

Riff 2

B D C♯ C | B D C♯ C | B D C♯ C

Copyright © 1973 by EXPERIENCE HENDRIX, L.L.C.
Copyright Renewed 2001
All Rights Controlled and Administered by EXPERIENCE HENDRIX, L.L.C.
All Rights Reserved

B D C♯ C E G F♯ F E G F♯ F
B D C♯ C B D C♯ C F♯ A G♯ G
E G F♯ F B D C♯ C B D C♯ C
Riff 3
B7 3 E7 B7
F♯7 E7 B7
Riff 4
B7 3 E7 B7
F♯7 E7 B7
Play 3 times
Guitar Solo 2/Riff 4
B7 3 E7 B7
F♯7 E7 B7
Outro
B7 2
Play 3 times

CD TRACK

4 Full Stereo Mix

12 Split Mix

C Version

# Little Wing

Words and Music by
Jimi Hendrix

Copyright © 1968 by EXPERIENCE HENDRIX, L.L.C.
Copyright Renewed 1996
All Rights Controlled and Administered by EXPERIENCE HENDRIX, L.L.C.
All Rights Reserved

G
Am
Em
WITH A THOU - SAND SMILES
SHE GIVES TO ME FREE.
Bm
B♭
Am
C
IT'S AL - RIGHT, SHE SAID. IT'S AL-RIGHT.
TAKE AN - Y - THING YOU WANT
G
Fadd9
C
FROM ME.
AN - Y - THING.
Guitar Solo
D
Em
AN - Y - THING.
G
Am
Em
FLY ON. LIT-TLE WING.
Bm B♭ Am C G Fadd9 C D
Outro
Em
G
Am
Em
YEAH, YEAH, YEAH, LIT-TLE WING.
Bm B♭ Am C G Fadd9 C D

**CD TRACK**

5 Full Stereo Mix

13 Split Mix

𝄢 C Version

# Red House

Words and Music by
Jimi Hendrix

Intro

Moderately slow Blues ♩. = 66

B7 B°7 B N.C.

Ah, ___ yeah! _

E7 B7

F#7 E7 B7 E7 E#7 F#7

1. There's a red

𝄋 Verse

B7 E7

house ___ o - ver yon - der, that's where my ba - by ___ stays.

See additional lyrics

B7 2 E7

Lord, there's a red house _ o - ver yon - der, _

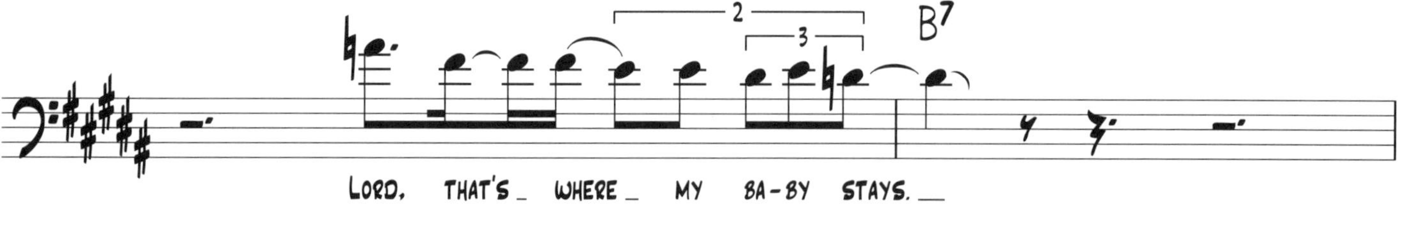

Copyright © 1967, 1968, 1980 by EXPERIENCE HENDRIX, L.L.C.
Copyright Renewed 1995, 1996
All Rights Controlled and Administered by EXPERIENCE HENDRIX, L.L.C.
All Rights Reserved

Additional Lyrics

2. Wait a minute, something's wrong here.
The key won't unlock the door.
Wait a minute, something's wrong.
Lord, have mercy, this key won't unlock this door.
Something's goin' wrong here.
I have a bad, bad feeling
That my baby don't live here no more.
That's alright, I still got my guitar. Look out now!
Yeah! That's alright!

3. Well, I might as well go back over yonder,
Way back among the hills.
Yeah, that's what I'm gonna do.
Lord, I might as well go back over yonder,
Way back yonder 'cross the hills.
'Cause if my baby don't love me no more,
I know her sister will!
Yeah!

Copyright © 1968 by EXPERIENCE HENDRIX, L.L.C.
Copyright Renewed 1996
All Rights Controlled and Administered by EXPERIENCE HENDRIX, L.L.C.
All Rights Reserved

Additional Lyrics

2. The clouds are really low, and they overflow with cotton candy
and battlegrounds, red and brown.
But it's all in your mind, don't think your time on bad things.
Just float your little mind around. Look out! Ooh! Heh.

Hang on my darlin', yeah. Hang on if you wanna go.
It's a, hah, look at you girl, you make me laugh, it's a,
Just a little bit of Spanish castle magic.
Yeah baby, it's a, uh hah.

D.S. Hang on my darlin'. Hey. Hang on, hang on if you wanna go.
It's a, oh girl, heh, that's right baby. It's a,
A little bit of Spanish castle magic.
Hey, little bit of Spanish castle magic.

**CD TRACK**
7 Full Stereo Mix
15 Split Mix
C Version

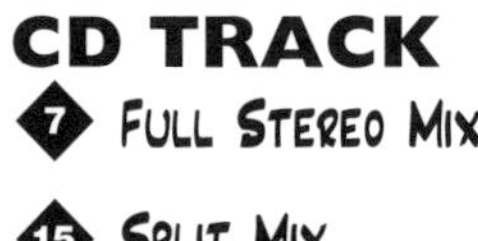

# Voodoo Child
## (Slight Return)

Words and Music by
Jimi Hendrix

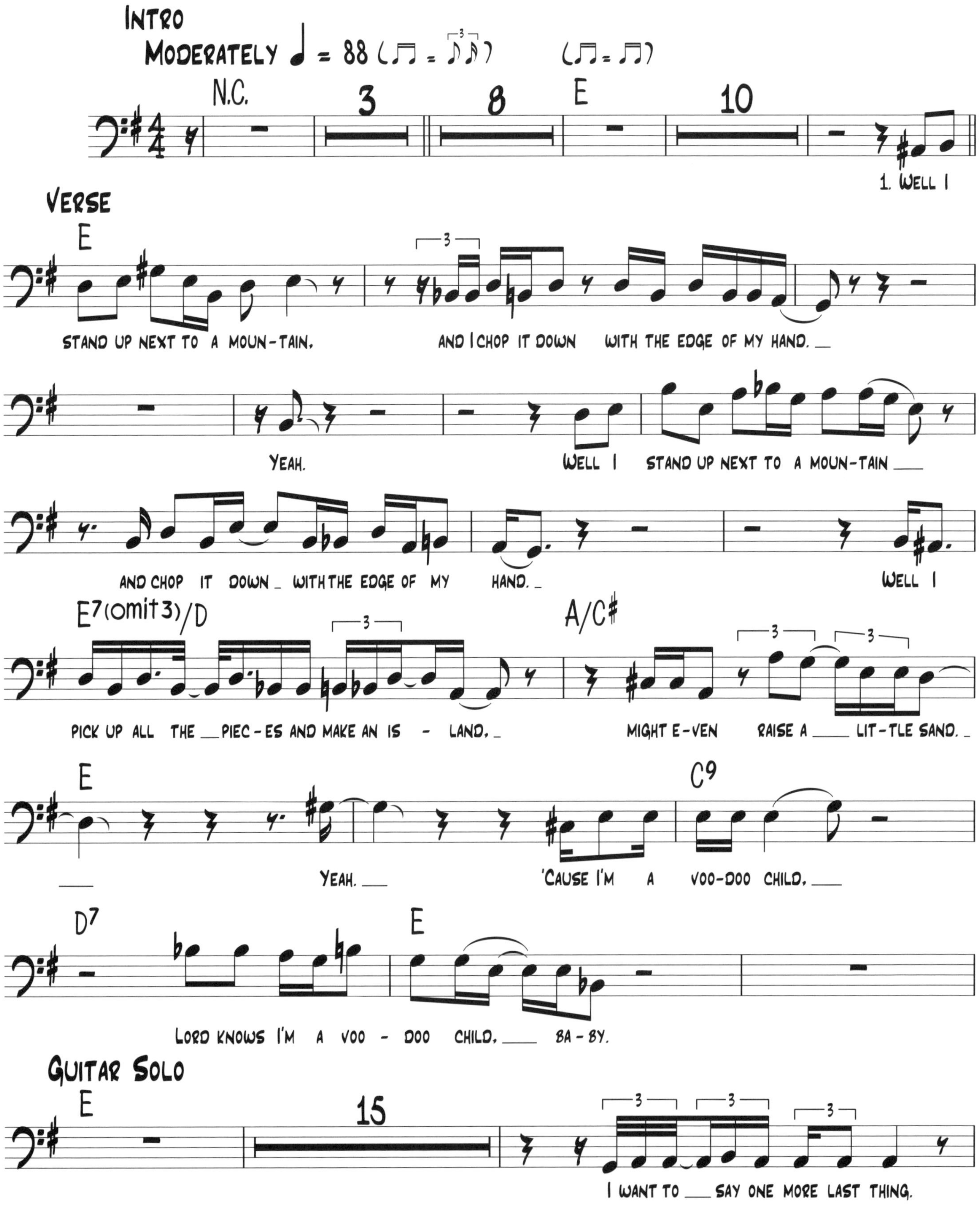
Intro
Moderately ♩ = 88
N.C.
3
8
E
10
1. Well I
Verse
E
stand up next to a moun-tain, and I chop it down with the edge of my hand.
Yeah.
Well I stand up next to a moun-tain
and chop it down with the edge of my hand.
Well I
E7(omit3)/D
pick up all the piec-es and make an is - land.
A/C#
might e-ven raise a lit-tle sand.
E
Yeah.
'Cause I'm a
C9
voo-doo child.
D7
Lord knows I'm a voo - doo
E
child, ba - by.
Guitar Solo
E
15
I want to say one more last thing.

Copyright © 1968, 1980 by EXPERIENCE HENDRIX, L.L.C.
Copyright Renewed 1996
All Rights Controlled and Administered by EXPERIENCE HENDRIX, L.L.C.
All Rights Reserved

Verse
E
2. I did-n't mean to take up all your sweet time.
I'll give it right back to you a one of these days.
Ha, ha, ha.
I said I did-n't mean to take up all your sweet time.
I'll give it right back one of these
days.
Yeah.
E7(omit3)/D
If I don't meet you no more in this world, then uh,
A/C#
E
E7
I'll meet you on the next one, and don't be late.
Don't be late.
'Cause I'm a
C7
D7
E
voo-doo child, voo-doo child,
Lord knows I'm a voo-doo child.
Hey.
Outro/Guitar Solo
E
hey, hey.
I'm a voo-doo child, ba by.
I don't take no for an an - swer.
ques - tion no.

**CD TRACK**

8 Full Stereo Mix

16 Split Mix

C Version

# Who Knows

Words and Music by
Jimi Hendrix

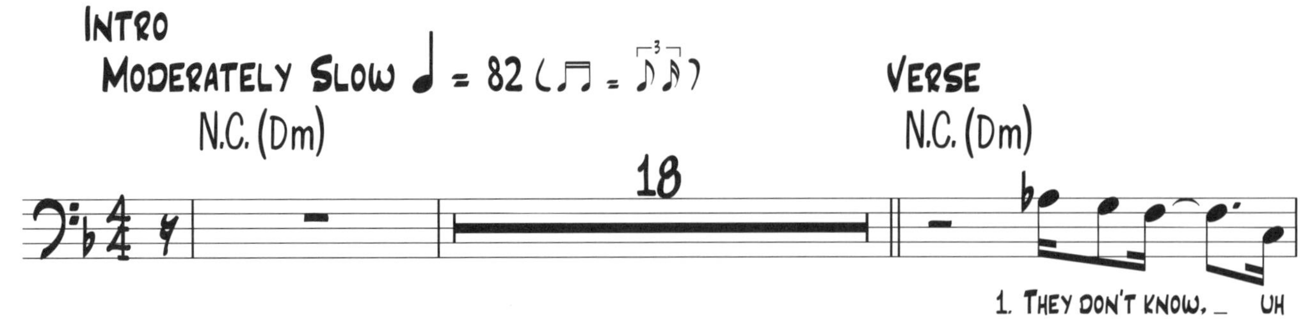

Copyright © 1970 by EXPERIENCE HENDRIX, L.L.C.
Copyright Renewed 1998
All Rights Controlled and Administered by EXPERIENCE HENDRIX, L.L.C.
All Rights Reserved

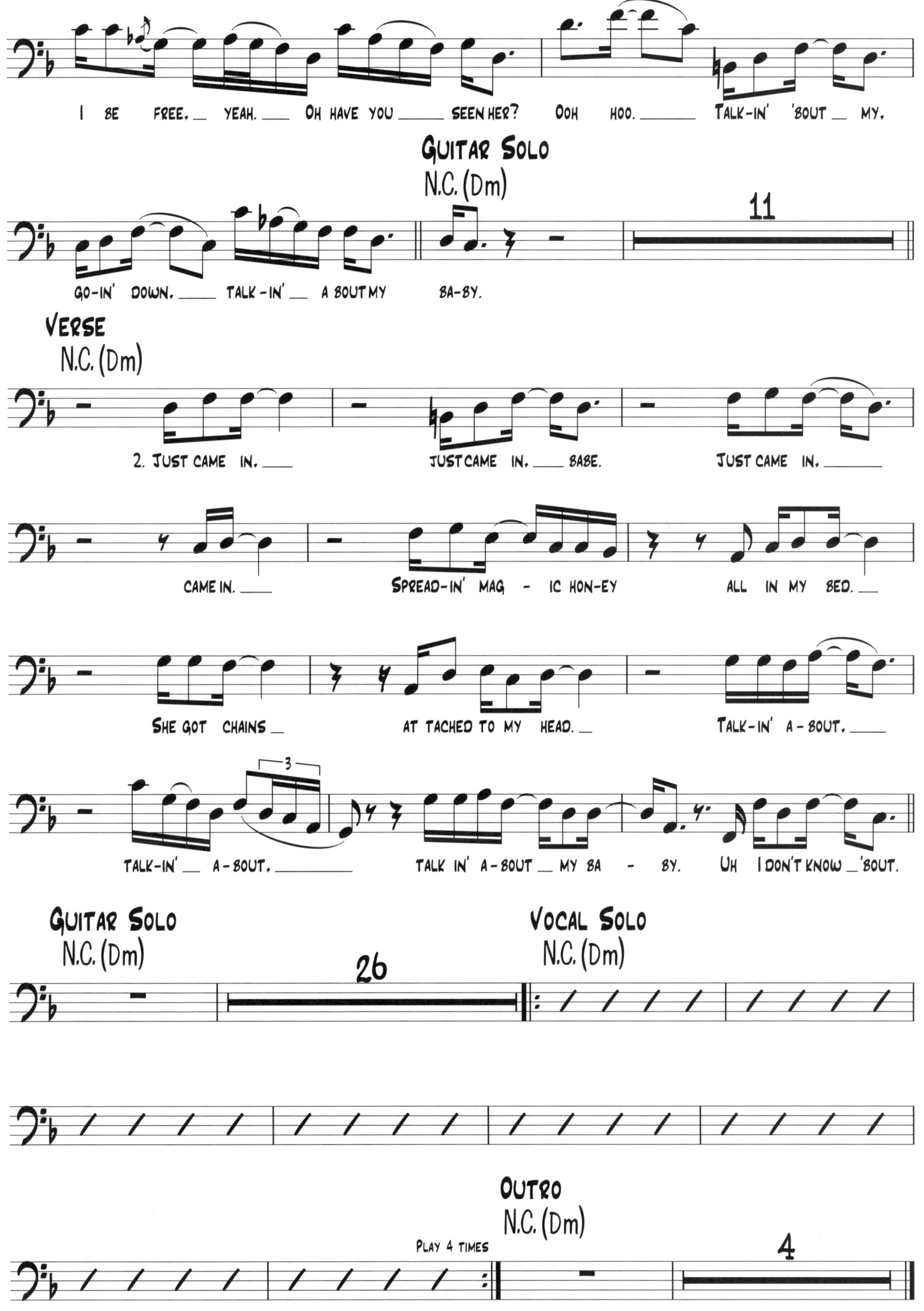

I BE FREE, YEAH. OH HAVE YOU SEEN HER? OOH HOO. TALK-IN' 'BOUT MY,
GUITAR SOLO
N.C. (Dm)
11
GO-IN' DOWN, TALK-IN' A BOUT MY BA-BY.
VERSE
N.C. (Dm)
2. JUST CAME IN, JUST CAME IN, BABE. JUST CAME IN,
CAME IN. SPREAD-IN' MAG - IC HON-EY ALL IN MY BED.
SHE GOT CHAINS AT TACHED TO MY HEAD. TALK-IN' A - BOUT,
3
TALK-IN' A - BOUT, TALK IN' A - BOUT MY BA - BY. UH I DON'T KNOW 'BOUT.
GUITAR SOLO
N.C. (Dm)
26
VOCAL SOLO
N.C. (Dm)
OUTRO
N.C. (Dm)
PLAY 4 TIMES
4

HAL•LEONARD

For use with all the C, B♭, Bass Clef and E♭ Instruments, the Hal Leonard Blues Play-Along Series is the ultimate jamming tool for all blues musicians.

With easy-to-read lead sheets, and other split-track choices on the included CD, these first-of-a-kind packages will bring your local blues jam right into your house! Each song on the CD includes two tracks: a full stereo mix, and a split track mix with removable guitar, bass, piano, and harp parts. The CD is playable on any CD player, and is also enhanced so Mac and PC users can adjust the recording to any tempo without changing the pitch!

**1. Chicago Blues**

All Your Love (I Miss Loving) • Easy Baby • I Ain't Got You • I'm Your Hoochie Coochie Man • Killing Floor • Mary Had a Little Lamb • Messin' with the Kid • Sweet Home Chicago.

00843106 Book/CD Pack ........................$12.99

**2. Texas Blues**

Hide Away • If You Love Me Like You Say • Mojo Hand • Okie Dokie Stomp • Pride and Joy • Reconsider Baby • T-Bone Shuffle • The Things That I Used to Do.

00843107 Book/CD Pack ........................$12.99

**3. Slow Blues**

Don't Throw Your Love on Me So Strong • Five Long Years • I Can't Quit You Baby • I Just Want to Make Love to You • The Sky Is Crying • (They Call It) Stormy Monday (Stormy Monday Blues) • Sweet Little Angel • Texas Flood.

00843108 Book/CD Pack ........................$12.99

**4. Shuffle Blues**

Beautician Blues • Bright Lights, Big City • Further on up the Road • I'm Tore Down • Juke • Let Me Love You Baby • Look at Little Sister • Rock Me Baby.

00843171 Book/CD Pack ........................$12.99

**5. B.B. King**

Everyday I Have the Blues • It's My Own Fault Darlin' • Just Like a Woman • Please Accept My Love • Sweet Sixteen • The Thrill Is Gone • Why I Sing the Blues • You Upset Me Baby.

00843172 Book/CD Pack ........................$14.99

**6. Jazz Blues**

Birk's Works • Blues in the Closet • Cousin Mary • Freddie Freeloader • Now's the Time • Tenor Madness • Things Ain't What They Used to Be • Turnaround.

00843175 Book/CD Pack ........................$12.99

**7. Howlin' Wolf**

Built for Comfort • Forty-Four • How Many More Years • Killing Floor • Moanin' at Midnight • Shake for Me • Sitting on Top of the World • Smokestack Lightning.

00843176 Book/CD Pack ........................$12.99

**8. Blues Classics**

Baby, Please Don't Go • Boom Boom • Born Under a Bad Sign • Dust My Broom • How Long, How Long Blues • I Ain't Superstitious • It Hurts Me Too • My Babe.

00843177 Book/CD Pack ........................$12.99

**9. Albert Collins**

Brick • Collins' Mix • Don't Lose Your Cool • Frost Bite • Frosty • I Ain't Drunk • Master Charge • Trash Talkin'.

00843178 Book/CD Pack ........................$12.99

**10. Uptempo Blues**

Cross Road Blues (Crossroads) • Give Me Back My Wig • Got My Mo Jo Working • The House Is Rockin' • Paying the Cost to Be the Boss • Rollin' and Tumblin' • Turn on Your Love Light • You Can't Judge a Book by the Cover.

00843179 Book/CD Pack ........................$12.99

**11. Christmas Blues**

Back Door Santa • Blue Christmas • Dig That Crazy Santa Claus • Merry Christmas, Baby • Please Come Home for Christmas • Santa Baby • Soulful Christmas.

00843203 Book/CD Pack ........................$12.99

**12. Jimmy Reed**

Ain't That Lovin' You Baby • Baby, What You Want Me to Do • Big Boss Man • Bright Lights, Big City • Going to New York • Honest I Do • You Don't Have to Go • You Got Me Dizzy.

00843204 Book/CD Pack ........................$12.99

FOR MORE INFORMATION, SEE YOUR LOCAL MUSIC DEALER, OR WRITE TO:

7777 W. BLUEMOUND RD. P.O. BOX 13819 MILWAUKEE, WI 53213

Prices, content, and availability subject to change without notice.

www.halleonard.com

# The Best-Selling Jazz Book of All Time Is Now Legal!

The Real Books are the most popular jazz books of all time. Since the 1970s, musicians have trusted these volumes to get them through every gig, night after night. The problem is that the books were illegally produced and distributed, without any regard to copyright law, or royalties paid to the composers who created these musical masterpieces.

Hal Leonard is very proud to present the first legitimate and legal editions of these books ever produced. You won't even notice the difference, other than all the notorious errors being fixed: the covers and typeface look the same, the song lists are nearly identical, and the price for our edition is even cheaper than the originals!

Every conscientious musician will appreciate that these books are now produced accurately and ethically, benefitting the songwriters that we owe for some of the greatest tunes of all time!

**VOLUME 1**

| | | |
|---|---|---|
| 00240221 | C Edition | $35.00 |
| 00240224 | B♭ Edition | $35.00 |
| 00240225 | E♭ Edition | $35.00 |
| 00240226 | Bass Clef Edition | $35.00 |
| 00240292 | C Edition 6 x 9 | $30.00 |
| 00240339 | B♭ Edition 6 x 9 | $30.00 |
| 00451087 | C Edition on CD-ROM | $25.00 |
| 00240302 | A-D CD Backing Tracks | $24.99 |
| 00240303 | E-J CD Backing Tracks | $24.95 |
| 00240304 | L-R CD Backing Tracks | $24.95 |
| 00240305 | S-Z CD Backing Tracks | $24.99 |
| 00110604 | Book/USB Flash Drive Backing Tracks Pack | $79.99 |
| 00110599 | USB Flash Drive Only | $50.00 |

**VOLUME 2**

| | | |
|---|---|---|
| 00240222 | C Edition | $35.50 |
| 00240227 | B♭ Edition | $35.00 |
| 00240228 | E♭ Edition | $35.00 |
| 00240229 | Bass Clef Edition | $35.00 |
| 00240293 | C Edition 6 x 9 | $27.95 |
| 00451088 | C Edition on CD-ROM | $27.99 |
| 00240351 | A-D CD Backing Tracks | $24.99 |
| 00240352 | E-I CD Backing Tracks | $24.99 |
| 00240353 | J-R CD Backing Tracks | $24.99 |
| 00240354 | S-Z CD Backing Tracks | $24.99 |

**VOLUME 3**

| | | |
|---|---|---|
| 00240233 | C Edition | $35.00 |
| 00240284 | B♭ Edition | $35.00 |
| 00240285 | E♭ Edition | $35.00 |
| 00240286 | Bass Clef Edition | $35.00 |
| 00240338 | C Edition 6 x 9 | $30.00 |
| 00451089 | C Edition on CD-ROM | $29.99 |

**VOLUME 4**

| | | |
|---|---|---|
| 00240296 | C Edition | $35.00 |
| 00103348 | B♭ Edition | $35.00 |
| 00103349 | E♭ Edition | $35.00 |
| 00103350 | Bass Clef Edition | $35.00 |

**VOLUME 5**

| | | |
|---|---|---|
| 00240349 | C Edition | $35.00 |

***Also available:***

| | | |
|---|---|---|
| 00240264 | The Real Blues Book | $34.99 |
| 00310910 | The Real Bluegrass Book | $29.99 |
| 00240137 | Miles Davis Real Book | $19.95 |
| 00240355 | The Real Dixieland Book | $29.99 |
| 00240235 | The Duke Ellington Real Book | $19.99 |
| 00240348 | The Real Latin Book | $35.00 |
| 00240358 | The Charlie Parker Real Book | $19.99 |
| 00240331 | The Bud Powell Real Book | $19.99 |
| 00240313 | The Real Rock Book | $35.00 |
| 00240323 | The Real Rock Book – Vol. 2 | $35.00 |
| 00240359 | The Real Tab Book – Vol. 1 | $32.50 |
| 00240317 | The Real Worship Book | $29.99 |

**THE REAL CHRISTMAS BOOK**

| | | |
|---|---|---|
| 00240306 | C Edition | $27.50 |
| 00240345 | B♭ Edition | $27.50 |
| 00240346 | E♭ Edition | $27.50 |
| 00240347 | Bass Clef Edition | $27.50 |
| 00240431 | A-G CD Backing Tracks | $24.99 |
| 00240432 | H-M CD Backing Tracks | $24.99 |
| 00240433 | N-Y CD Backing Tracks | $24.99 |

**THE REAL VOCAL BOOK**

| | | |
|---|---|---|
| 00240230 | Volume 1 High Voice | $35.00 |
| 00240307 | Volume 1 Low Voice | $35.00 |
| 00240231 | Volume 2 High Voice | $35.00 |
| 00240308 | Volume 2 Low Voice | $35.00 |
| 00240391 | Volume 3 High Voice | $29.99 |
| 00240392 | Volume 3 Low Voice | $35.00 |

**THE REAL BOOK – STAFF PAPER**

00240327 .......... $9.95

**HOW TO PLAY FROM A REAL BOOK**
FOR ALL MUSICIANS
*by Robert Rawlins*
00312097 .......... $17.50

**Complete song lists online at www.halleonard.com**

*Prices, content, and availability subject to change without notice.*

7777 W. BLUEMOUND RD. P.O. BOX 13819 MILWAUKEE, WI 53213

0313

# Presenting the Hal Leonard JAZZ PLAY-ALONG SERIES

For use with all B-flat, E-flat, Bass Clef and C instruments, the Jazz Play-Along® Series is the ultimate learning tool for all jazz musicians. With musician-friendly lead sheets, melody cues, and other split-track choices on the included CD, these first-of-a-kind packages help you master improvisation while playing some of the greatest tunes of all time. FOR STUDY, each tune includes a split track with: melody cue with proper style and inflection • professional rhythm tracks • choruses for soloing • removable bass part • removable piano part. FOR PERFORMANCE, each tune also has: an additional full stereo accompaniment track (no melody) • additional choruses for soloing.

**1A. MAIDEN VOYAGE/ALL BLUES**
00843158 ............ $15.99

**1. DUKE ELLINGTON**
00841644 ............ $16.95

**2. MILES DAVIS**
00841645 ............ $16.95

**3. THE BLUES**
00841646 ............ $16.99

**4. JAZZ BALLADS**
00841691 ............ $16.99

**5. BEST OF BEBOP**
00841689 ............ $16.95

**6. JAZZ CLASSICS WITH EASY CHANGES**
00841690 ............ $16.99

**7. ESSENTIAL JAZZ STANDARDS**
00843000 ............ $16.99

**8. ANTONIO CARLOS JOBIM AND THE ART OF THE BOSSA NOVA**
00843001 ............ $16.95

**9. DIZZY GILLESPIE**
00843002 ............ $16.99

**10. DISNEY CLASSICS**
00843003 ............ $16.99

**11. RODGERS AND HART FAVORITES**
00843004 ............ $16.99

**12. ESSENTIAL JAZZ CLASSICS**
00843005 ............ $16.99

**13. JOHN COLTRANE**
00843006 ............ $16.95

**14. IRVING BERLIN**
00843007 ............ $15.99

**15. RODGERS & HAMMERSTEIN**
00843008 ............ $15.99

**16. COLE PORTER**
00843009 ............ $15.95

**17. COUNT BASIE**
00843010 ............ $16.95

**18. HAROLD ARLEN**
00843011 ............ $15.95

**19. COOL JAZZ**
00843012 ............ $15.95

**20. CHRISTMAS CAROLS**
00843080 ............ $14.95

**21. RODGERS AND HART CLASSICS**
00843014 ............ $14.95

**22. WAYNE SHORTER**
00843015 ............ $16.95

**23. LATIN JAZZ**
00843016 ............ $16.95

**24. EARLY JAZZ STANDARDS**
00843017 ............ $14.95

**25. CHRISTMAS JAZZ**
00843018 ............ $16.95

**26. CHARLIE PARKER**
00843019 ............ $16.95

**27. GREAT JAZZ STANDARDS**
00843020 ............ $16.99

**28. BIG BAND ERA**
00843021 ............ $15.99

**29. LENNON AND MCCARTNEY**
00843022 ............ $16.95

**30. BLUES' BEST**
00843023 ............ $15.99

**31. JAZZ IN THREE**
00843024 ............ $15.99

**32. BEST OF SWING**
00843025 ............ $15.99

**33. SONNY ROLLINS**
00843029 ............ $15.95

**34. ALL TIME STANDARDS**
00843030 ............ $15.99

**35. BLUESY JAZZ**
00843031 ............ $16.99

**36. HORACE SILVER**
00843032 ............ $16.99

**37. BILL EVANS**
00843033 ............ $16.95

**38. YULETIDE JAZZ**
00843034 ............ $16.95

**39. "ALL THE THINGS YOU ARE" & MORE JEROME KERN SONGS**
00843035 ............ $15.99

**40. BOSSA NOVA**
00843036 ............ $16.99

**41. CLASSIC DUKE ELLINGTON**
00843037 ............ $16.99

**42. GERRY MULLIGAN FAVORITES**
00843038 ............ $16.99

**43. GERRY MULLIGAN CLASSICS**
00843039 ............ $16.99

**44. OLIVER NELSON**
00843040 ............ $16.95

**45. GEORGE GERSHWIN**
00103643 ............ $24.99

**46. BROADWAY JAZZ STANDARDS**
00843042 ............ $15.99

**47. CLASSIC JAZZ BALLADS**
00843043 ............ $15.99

**48. BEBOP CLASSICS**
00843044 ............ $16.99

**49. MILES DAVIS STANDARDS**
00843045 ............ $16.95

**50. GREAT JAZZ CLASSICS**
00843046 ............ $15.99

**51. UP-TEMPO JAZZ**
00843047 ............ $15.99

**52. STEVIE WONDER**
00843048 ............ $16.99

**53. RHYTHM CHANGES**
00843049 ............ $15.99

**54. "MOONLIGHT IN VERMONT" AND OTHER GREAT STANDARDS**
00843050 ............ $15.99

**55. BENNY GOLSON**
00843052 ............ $15.95

**56. "GEORGIA ON MY MIND" & OTHER SONGS BY HOAGY CARMICHAEL**
00843056 ............ $15.99

**57. VINCE GUARALDI**
00843057 ............ $16.99

**58. MORE LENNON AND MCCARTNEY**
00843059 ............ $16.99

**59. SOUL JAZZ**
00843060 ............ $16.99

**60. DEXTER GORDON**
00843061 ............ $15.95

**61. MONGO SANTAMARIA**
00843062 ............ $15.95

**62. JAZZ-ROCK FUSION**
00843063 ............ $16.99

**63. CLASSICAL JAZZ**
00843064 ............ $14.95

**64. TV TUNES**
00843065 ............ $14.95

**65. SMOOTH JAZZ**
00843066 ............ $16.99

**66. A CHARLIE BROWN CHRISTMAS**
00843067 $16.99

**67. CHICK COREA**
00843068 $15.95

**68. CHARLES MINGUS**
00843069 $16.95

**69. CLASSIC JAZZ**
00843071 $15.99

**70. THE DOORS**
00843072 $14.95

**71. COLE PORTER CLASSICS**
00843073 $14.95

**72. CLASSIC JAZZ BALLADS**
00843074 $15.99

**73. JAZZ/BLUES**
00843075 $14.95

**74. BEST JAZZ CLASSICS**
00843076 $15.99

**75. PAUL DESMOND**
00843077 $16.99

**76. BROADWAY JAZZ BALLADS**
00843078 $15.99

**77. JAZZ ON BROADWAY**
00843079 $15.99

**78. STEELY DAN**
00843070 $15.99

**79. MILES DAVIS CLASSICS**
00843081 $15.99

**80. JIMI HENDRIX**
00843083 $16.99

**81. FRANK SINATRA – CLASSICS**
00843084 $15.99

**82. FRANK SINATRA – STANDARDS**
00843085 $16.99

**83. ANDREW LLOYD WEBBER**
00843104 $14.95

**84. BOSSA NOVA CLASSICS**
00843105 $14.95

**85. MOTOWN HITS**
00843109 $14.95

**86. BENNY GOODMAN**
00843110 $15.99

**87. DIXIELAND**
00843111 $16.99

**88. DUKE ELLINGTON FAVORITES**
00843112 $14.95

**89. IRVING BERLIN FAVORITES**
00843113 $14.95

**90. THELONIOUS MONK CLASSICS**
00841262 $16.99

**91. THELONIOUS MONK FAVORITES**
00841263 $16.99

**92. LEONARD BERNSTEIN**
00450134 $15.99

**93. DISNEY FAVORITES**
00843142 $14.99

**94. RAY**
00843143 $14.99

**95. JAZZ AT THE LOUNGE**
00843144 $14.99

**96. LATIN JAZZ STANDARDS**
00843145 $15.99

**97. MAYBE I'M AMAZED***
00843148 $15.99

**98. DAVE FRISHBERG**
00843149 $15.99

**99. SWINGING STANDARDS**
00843150 $14.99

**100. LOUIS ARMSTRONG**
00740423 $16.99

**101. BUD POWELL**
00843152 $14.99

**102. JAZZ POP**
00843153 $15.99

**103. ON GREEN DOLPHIN STREET & OTHER JAZZ CLASSICS**
00843154 $14.99

**104. ELTON JOHN**
00843155 $14.99

**105. SOULFUL JAZZ**
00843151 $15.99

**106. SLO' JAZZ**
00843117 $14.99

**107. MOTOWN CLASSICS**
00843116 $14.99

**108. JAZZ WALTZ**
00843159 $15.99

**109. OSCAR PETERSON**
00843160 $16.99

**110. JUST STANDARDS**
00843161 $15.99

**111. COOL CHRISTMAS**
00843162 $15.99

**112. PAQUITO D'RIVERA – LATIN JAZZ***
48020662 $16.99

**113. PAQUITO D'RIVERA – BRAZILIAN JAZZ***
48020663 $19.99

**114. MODERN JAZZ QUARTET FAVORITES**
00843163 $15.99

**115. THE SOUND OF MUSIC**
00843164 $15.99

**116. JACO PASTORIUS**
00843165 $15.99

**117. ANTONIO CARLOS JOBIM – MORE HITS**
00843166 $15.99

**118. BIG JAZZ STANDARDS COLLECTION**
00843167 $27.50

**119. JELLY ROLL MORTON**
00843168 $15.99

**120. J.S. BACH**
00843169 $15.99

**121. DJANGO REINHARDT**
00843170 $15.99

**122. PAUL SIMON**
00843182 $16.99

**123. BACHARACH & DAVID**
00843185 $15.99

**124. JAZZ-ROCK HORN HITS**
00843186 $15.99

**126. COUNT BASIE CLASSICS**
00843157 $15.99

**127. CHUCK MANGIONE**
00843188 $15.99

**128. VOCAL STANDARDS (LOW VOICE)**
00843189 $15.99

**129. VOCAL STANDARDS (HIGH VOICE)**
00843190 $15.99

**130. VOCAL JAZZ (LOW VOICE)**
00843191 $15.99

**131. VOCAL JAZZ (HIGH VOICE)**
00843192 $15.99

**132. STAN GETZ ESSENTIALS**
00843193 $15.99

**133. STAN GETZ FAVORITES**
00843194 $15.99

**134. NURSERY RHYMES***
00843196 $17.99

**135. JEFF BECK**
00843197 $15.99

**136. NAT ADDERLEY**
00843198 $15.99

**137. WES MONTGOMERY**
00843199 $15.99

**138. FREDDIE HUBBARD**
00843200 $15.99

**139. JULIAN "CANNONBALL" ADDERLEY**
00843201 $15.99

**140. JOE ZAWINUL**
00843202 $15.99

**141. BILL EVANS STANDARDS**
00843156 $15.99

**142. CHARLIE PARKER GEMS**
00843222 $15.99

**143. JUST THE BLUES**
00843223 $15.99

**144. LEE MORGAN**
00843229 $15.99

**145. COUNTRY STANDARDS**
00843230 $15.99

**146. RAMSEY LEWIS**
00843231 $15.99

**147. SAMBA**
00843232 $15.99

**150. JAZZ IMPROV BASICS**
00843195 $19.99

**151. MODERN JAZZ QUARTET CLASSICS**
00843209 $15.99

**152. J.J. JOHNSON**
00843210 $15.99

**154. HENRY MANCINI**
00843213 $14.99

**155. SMOOTH JAZZ CLASSICS**
00843215 $15.99

**156. THELONIOUS MONK – EARLY GEMS**
00843216 $15.99

**157. HYMNS**
00843217 $15.99

**158. JAZZ COVERS ROCK**
00843219 $15.99

**159. MOZART**
00843220 $15.99

**160. GEORGE SHEARING**
14041531 $16.99

**161. DAVE BRUBECK**
14041556 $16.99

**162. BIG CHRISTMAS COLLECTION**
00843221 $24.99

**164. HERB ALPERT**
14041775 $16.99

**165. GEORGE BENSON**
00843240 $16.99

**168. TADD DAMERON**
00103663 $15.99

**169. BEST JAZZ STANDARDS**
00109249 $19.99

*These CDs do not include split tracks.

Prices, contents, and availability subject to change without notice.

HAL•LEONARD®
CORPORATION
7777 W. BLUEMOUND RD. P.O. BOX 13819
MILWAUKEE, WISCONSIN 53213

For complete songlists and more, visit Hal Leonard online at
**www.halleonard.com**

# ARTIST TRANSCRIPTIONS®

**Artist Transcriptions** are authentic, note-for-note transcriptions of today's hottest artists in jazz, pop and rock. These outstanding, accurate arrangements are in an easy-to-read format which includes all essential lines. **Artist Transcriptions** can be used to perform, sequence or for reference.

## CLARINET

00672423 Buddy De Franco Collection ........ $19.95

## FLUTE

00672379 Eric Dolphy Collection ........ $19.95
00672582 The Very Best of James Galway ........ $16.99
00672372 James Moody Collection – Sax and Flute ........ $19.95
00660108 James Newton – Improvising Flute ........ $14.95

## GUITAR & BASS

00660113 The Guitar Style of George Benson ........ $14.95
00699072 Guitar Book of Pierre Bensusan ........ $29.95
00672331 Ron Carter – Acoustic Bass ........ $16.95
00672307 Stanley Clarke Collection ........ $19.95
00660115 Al Di Meola – Friday Night in San Francisco ........ $14.95
00604043 Al Di Meola – Music, Words, Pictures ........ $14.95
00672574 Al Di Meola – Pursuit of Radical Rhapsody ........ $22.99
00673245 Jazz Style of Tal Farlow ........ $19.95
00672359 Bela Fleck and the Flecktones ........ $18.95
00699389 Jim Hall – Jazz Guitar Environments ........ $19.95
00699306 Jim Hall – Exploring Jazz Guitar ........ $19.95
00604049 Allan Holdsworth – Reaching for the Uncommon Chord ........ $14.95
00699215 Leo Kottke – Eight Songs ........ $14.95
00675536 Wes Montgomery – Guitar Transcriptions ........ $17.95
00672353 Joe Pass Collection ........ $18.95
00673216 John Patitucci ........ $16.95
00027083 Django Reinhardt Antholog ........ $14.95
00026711 Genius of Django Reinhardt ........ $10.95
00672374 Johnny Smith Guitar Solos ........ $19.99
00672320 Mark Whitfield ........ $19.95

## PIANO & KEYBOARD

00672338 Monty Alexander Collection ........ $19.95
00672487 Monty Alexander Plays Standards ........ $19.95
00672520 Count Basie Collection ........ $19.95
00672439 Cyrus Chestnut Collection ........ $19.95
00672300 Chick Corea – Paint the World ........ $12.95
00672537 Bill Evans at Town Hall ........ $16.95
00672548 The Mastery of Bill Evans ........ $12.95
00672425 Bill Evans – Piano Interpretations ........ $19.95
00672365 Bill Evans – Piano Standards ........ $19.95
00672510 Bill Evans Trio – Vol. 1: 1959-1961 ........ $24.95
00672511 Bill Evans Trio – Vol. 2: 1962-1965 ........ $24.95
00672512 Bill Evans Trio – Vol. 3: 1968-1974 ........ $24.95
00672513 Bill Evans Trio – Vol. 4: 1979-1980 ........ $24.95
00672381 Tommy Flanagan Collection ........ $24.99
00672492 Benny Goodman Collection ........ $16.95
00672486 Vince Guaraldi Collection ........ $19.95
00672419 Herbie Hancock Collection ........ $19.95
00672438 Hampton Hawes ........ $19.95
00672322 Ahmad Jamal Collection ........ $22.95
00672564 Best of Jeff Lorber ........ $17.99
00672476 Brad Mehldau Collection ........ $19.99
00672388 Best of Thelonious Monk ........ $19.95
00672389 Thelonious Monk Collection ........ $19.95
00672390 Thelonious Monk Plays Jazz Standards – Volume 1 ........ $19.95
00672391 Thelonious Monk Plays Jazz Standards – Volume 2 ........ $19.95
00672433 Jelly Roll Morton – The Piano Rolls ........ $12.95
00672553 Charlie Parker for Piano ........ $19.95
00672542 Oscar Peterson – Jazz Piano Solos ........ $16.95
00672562 Oscar Peterson – A Jazz Portrait of Frank Sinatra ........ $19.95
00672544 Oscar Peterson – Originals ........ $9.95
00672532 Oscar Peterson – Plays Broadway ........ $19.95
00672531 Oscar Peterson – Plays Duke Ellington ........ $19.95
00672563 Oscar Peterson – A Royal Wedding Suite ........ $19.99
00672533 Oscar Peterson – Trios ........ $24.95
00672543 Oscar Peterson Trio – Canadiana Suite ........ $10.99
00672534 Very Best of Oscar Peterson ........ $22.95
00672371 Bud Powell Classics ........ $19.95
00672376 Bud Powell Collection ........ $19.95
00672437 André Previn Collection ........ $19.95
00672507 Gonzalo Rubalcaba Collection ........ $19.95
00672303 Horace Silver Collection ........ $19.95
00672316 Art Tatum Collection ........ $22.95
00672355 Art Tatum Solo Book ........ $19.95
00672357 Billy Taylor Collection ........ $24.95
00673215 McCoy Tyner ........ $16.95
00672321 Cedar Walton Collection ........ $19.95
00672519 Kenny Werner Collection ........ $19.95
00672434 Teddy Wilson Collection ........ $19.95

## SAXOPHONE

00672566 The Mindi Abair Collection ........ $14.99
00673244 Julian "Cannonball" Adderley Collection ........ $19.95
00673237 Michael Brecker ........ $19.95
00672429 Michael Brecker Collection ........ $19.95
00672315 Benny Carter Plays Standards ........ $22.95
00672314 Benny Carter Collection ........ $22.95
00672394 James Carter Collection ........ $19.95
00672349 John Coltrane Plays Giant Steps ........ $19.95
00672529 John Coltrane – Giant Steps ........ $14.99
00672494 John Coltrane – A Love Supreme ........ $14.95
00307393 John Coltrane – Omnibook: C Instruments ........ $19.99
00307391 John Coltrane – Omnibook: B-flat Instruments ........ $19.99
00307392 John Coltrane – Omnibook: E-flat Instruments ........ $19.99
00307394 John Coltrane – Omnibook: Bass Clef Instruments ........ $19.99
00672493 John Coltrane Plays "Coltrane Changes" ........ $19.95
00672453 John Coltrane Plays Standards ........ $19.95
00673233 John Coltrane Solos ........ $22.95
00672328 Paul Desmond Collection ........ $19.95
00672379 Eric Dolphy Collection ........ $19.95
00672530 Kenny Garrett Collection ........ $19.95
00699375 Stan Getz ........ $19.95
00672377 Stan Getz – Bossa Novas ........ $19.95
00672375 Stan Getz – Standards ........ $18.95
00673254 Great Tenor Sax Solos ........ $18.95
00672523 Coleman Hawkins Collection ........ $19.95
00673252 Joe Henderson – Selections from "Lush Life" & "So Near So Far" ........ $19.95
00672330 Best of Joe Henderson ........ $22.95
00672350 Tenor Saxophone Standards ........ $18.95
00673239 Best of Kenny G ........ $19.95
00673229 Kenny G – Breathless ........ $19.95
00672462 Kenny G – Classics in the Key of G ........ $19.95
00672485 Kenny G – Faith: A Holiday Album ........ $14.95
00672373 Kenny G – The Moment ........ $19.95
00672326 Joe Lovano Collection ........ $19.95
00672498 Jackie McLean Collection ........ $19.95
00672372 James Moody Collection – Sax and Flute ........ $19.95
00672416 Frank Morgan Collection ........ $19.95
00672539 Gerry Mulligan Collection ........ $19.95
00672352 Charlie Parker Collection ........ $19.95
00672561 Best of Sonny Rollins ........ $19.95
00672444 Sonny Rollins Collection ........ $19.95
00102751 Sonny Rollins with the Modern Jazz Quartet ........ $17.99
00675000 David Sanborn Collection ........ $17.95
00672528 Bud Shank Collection ........ $19.95
00672491 New Best of Wayne Shorter ........ $19.95
00672550 The Sonny Stitt Collection ........ $19.95
00672350 Tenor Saxophone Standards ........ $18.95
00672567 The Best of Kim Waters ........ $17.99
00672524 Lester Young Collection ........ $19.95

## TROMBONE

00672332 J.J. Johnson Collection ........ $19.95
00672489 Steve Turré Collection ........ $19.99

## TRUMPET

00672557 Herb Alpert Collection ........ $14.99
00672480 Louis Armstrong Collection ........ $17.95
00672481 Louis Armstrong Plays Standards ........ $17.95
00672435 Chet Baker Collection ........ $19.95
00672556 Best of Chris Botti ........ $19.95
00672448 Miles Davis – Originals, Vol. 1 ........ $19.95
00672451 Miles Davis – Originals, Vol. 2 ........ $19.95
00672450 Miles Davis – Standards, Vol. 1 ........ $19.95
00672449 Miles Davis – Standards, Vol. 2 ........ $19.95
00672479 Dizzy Gillespie Collection ........ $19.95
00673214 Freddie Hubbard ........ $14.95
00672382 Tom Harrell – Jazz Trumpet ........ $19.95
00672363 Jazz Trumpet Solos ........ $9.95
00672506 Chuck Mangione Collection ........ $19.95
00672525 Arturo Sandoval – Trumpet Evolution ........ $19.95

7777 W. BLUEMOUND RD. P.O. BOX 13819 MILWAUKEE, WI 53213

Visit our web site for a complete listing of our titles with songlists at
**www.halleonard.com**

Prices and availability subject to change without notice.

0113